CITYPACK GUIDE TO
Hong Kong

D0182866

How to Use This Book

KEY TO SYMBOLS

⊕ Map reference to the accompanying fold-out map

✉ Address

☎ Telephone number

🕐 Opening/closing times

🍴 Restaurant or café

🚆 Nearest rail station

🚇 Nearest subway or MTR (Mass Transit Railway) station

🚌 Nearest bus route

⛴ Nearest riverboat or ferry stop

♿ Facilities for visitors with disabilities

❓ Other practical information

▷ Further information

ℹ Tourist information

✋ Admission charges: Expensive (more than HK$200) Moderate (HK$50–HK$200 Inexpensive (HK$50 or less)

This guide is divided into four sections
• Essential Hong Kong: An introduction to the city and tips on making the most of your stay.
• Hong Kong by Area: We've broken the city into four areas, and recommended the best sights, shops, entertainment venues, nightlife and restaurants in each one. Suggested walks help you to explore on foot.
• Where to Stay: The best hotels, whether you're looking for luxury, budget or something in between.
• Need to Know: The info you need to make your trip run smoothly, including getting about by public transport, weather tips, emergency phone numbers and useful websites.

Navigation In the Hong Kong by Area chapter, we've given each area its own color, which is also used on the locator maps throughout the book and the map on the inside front cover.

Maps The fold-out map accompanying this book is a comprehensive street plan of central Hong Kong. The grid on this map is the same as the grid on the Hong Kong Island and Kowloon area locator maps and has upper case grid references. Sights and listings within the New Territories area have lower case grid references.

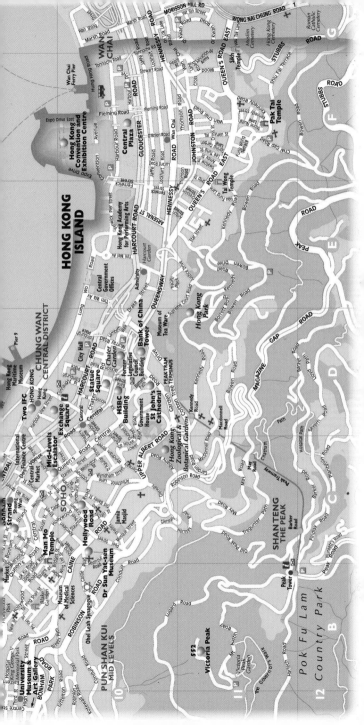

Contents

CONTENTS

Introducing Hong Kong

Amid the heat and bustle of the Asian tropics, Hong Kong stands in glass and steel. For a century and a half, this city of seven million has been extending a welcome to guests charmed by its beguiling mix of macho western capitalism and eastern mores.

From earliest colonial days, the wild islands, bays and mountains have been part of the appeal, but the modern focus tends toward the man-made. Designer shops, restaurants and trendy clubs have taken root within the urban jungle. Looking down at it all after dark from Victoria Peak is nothing short of metropolis-shaped seduction.

The ride has been turbulent since 1997. At first there was economic uncertainty and population shifts. The Asian Financial Crisis hit just as the British sailed out, bird flu and SARS drove tourists away, and protests erupted over political interference from Beijing. Things have sometimes seemed shaky. Hong Kongers, however, are a special breed—resilient, hard working. They embrace Western ideas but traditional Chinese culture is strong. The Special Administrative Region of Hong Kong had a difficult first decade, but these difficulties have made it stronger. You'll see people in the parks practising t'ai chi, the ancient, elegant exercise routines as often as you'll see a string of joggers.

In amongst the melee, Hong Kong rebranded itself as one of the most dynamic economics and cultures in the world. Newly moneyed China has forced Hong Kong to reassess its sense of superiority, but the booming mainland tourist trade has driven glitzy new developments in hotels, restaurants and infrastructure.

Modern Hong Kong society has money on its mind but it's combined with cultural savvy and a global outlook. Hong Kong has had its challenges in its near-two decades of independent rule, but it's survived them all to emerge more vibrant than ever.

Facts + Figures

- Hong Kong has a population of 7 million.
- 80 percent of Hong Kong's territory is rural or country park.
- Since the first reclamation project began in the 1850s, some 27sq miles (70sq km) of new land has been created.

WORKING TOGETHER

Mainland Chinese have been blamed for everything from inflating property prices to overburdening the health system and causing some food shortages. Called "locust" by some, even curmudgeons would admit that the mainland has been vital to the city's economic revival. There's a reason why young Hong Kongers can speak Mandarin, the mainland lingo.

BEGINNINGS

After being ceded to the British in 1842, Hong Kong Island thrived as a colonial trading hub. Jardine, Matheson and Co. dominated business, working initially in tea, cotton and opium. Clippers from India were spied from Jardine's Lookout, a peak above Causeway Bay, sometimes alongside chasing pirates. Indeed, the Noonday Gun, a surviving canon, was originally one of the campany's anti-piracy safeguards.

SOFT SKILLS

China's post-1980s opening up means Hong Kong is no longer the vital stepping stone for trade between East and West. However, it's remained king in the soft services of globalization—finance and insurance—and has worked hard to attract tourists from around the world. Despite the frenetic pace and tropical heat, Hong Kongers are unfailingly polite, friendly and welcoming.

A Short Stay in Hong Kong

DAY 1

Morning After a buffet breakfast in your hotel head straight for the **Peak** (▷ 38–39) taking the Peak tram to view the city and its islands stretched out before you. There are 360-degree views from the Sky Terrace at the top of the Peak Tower.

Mid-morning Back down in Central head for **Cat Street** (▷ 44) where antiques and bric-a-brac fill the markets; load up with gifts and curiosities.

Lunch Enjoy a good-value set lunch at one of the trendy diners along Elgin Street.

Afternoon What better way to experience the real Hong Kong than to take a ride on the **Star Ferry** (▷ 60–61) to Kowloon where you can take in the museums of the Tsim Sha Tsui Waterfront or indulge in a little retail therapy on Nathan or Canton roads.

Mid-afternoon For a break from shopping, try afternoon tea at the **InterContinental** lobby lounge (▷ 112) with its quiet luxury and spectacular views of the harbor.

Dinner Before dinner make sure you're at the clock tower at 8pm to watch the nightly **Symphony of Lights** (▷ 62–63), which illuminates the harbor. For dinner, if you have managed to get a reservation go back to the island and try **Caprice** (▷ 48) where the superb cuisine, discreet service and art nouveau surroundings make for a memorable evening.

Evening Take the Mid-Levels escalator (an experience in itself) to SoHo for a few drinks in **Staunton's Wine Bar** (▷ 47). Then to Lan Kwai Fong for some fun in one of the many bars.

DAY 2

Morning Take the MTR Tung Chung line to **Lantau Island** (▷ 98–99). Here the first fun of the day begins with a 30-minute cable-car ride on Skyrail. Enjoy panoramic views before arriving at Ngong Ping Village, where you can wander around the outlets, take part in a tea ceremony, or experience the immersive Walking with Buddha exhibition.

Mid-morning Walk over to the **Tian Tan Buddha** (▷ 98–99), buy a meal coupon at the bottom of the stairs and head up to the Buddha and the museum inside.

Lunch Enjoy a vegetarian lunch at the **monastery** (▷ 98–99), or if you must eat meat hop back down to Ngong Ping to try the food outlets there.

Afternoon Head to Kowloon and make your way to **Ladies' Market** in Mong Kok (▷ 68), where you can try your hand at bargaining for inexpensive clothes. Stop by at the **Nelson Street Wetmarket**, where the produce is sold from buckets and tubs and filleted to order.

Mid-afternoon Don't forget to seek out the bird market in **Yuen Po Street** where you can watch the caged birds sing while their owners feed them crickets with chopsticks.

Dinner This time the area to choose has to be **Mong Kok** (▷ 68) for a real Chinese dinner. Try **Fu Wah** (▷ 75) in Viceroy Market, which comes highly recommended as one of the best inexpensive pork and rice restaurants in the city.

Evening Knutsford Terrace has a quieter, more local atmosphere than Soho or Lan Kwai Fong, and has bars to suit all tastes.

▼
▼
▼
Aberdeen (▷ 24–25)
Visit one of the many
floating restaurants in
Aberdeen's harbor.

Central Plaza (▷ 26)
Enjoy bird's-eye views
from the 46th-floor
observation point.

**Cheung Chau Island
(▷ 94–95)** Explore the
hills and temples of
"Long Island."

**Hong Kong Disneyland
(▷ 96–97)** Fairy-tale
theme park on Lantau
Island.

Hong Kong Park (▷ 27)
Birds, lakes, plants and
waterfalls spread over
25 acres (10ha).

**Hong Kong Wetland
Park (▷ 80–81)** 151
acres (61ha) of natural and
landscaped parklands.

**Hong Kong Zoological
and Botanical Gardens
(▷ 28–29)** Escape from
the city in this paradise of
flora and fauna.

**Kowloon Walled City
Park (▷ 54)** An oasis of
calm in central Kowloon.

Man Mo Temple (▷ 30)
Hong Kong's oldest temple,
dedicated to Man and Mo.

**Mid-Levels Escalator
(▷ 31)** Mingle with the
commuter crowd.

Museum of Art (▷ 55)
Among the works on
display is the first known
painting of Hong Kong.

**Museum of History
(▷ 56)** Exhibits trace Hong
Kong's history.

Ocean Park (▷ 32–33)
One of southeast Asia's
largest amusement parks.

Science Museum (▷ 57)
Robots, virtual reality and
lots more hands-on
science projects.

**Space Museum (▷ 58–
59)** Don't miss seeing an
Omnimax film here.

Stanley (▷ 34–35)
Famous market, as well as
beaches and temples.

Star Ferry (▷ 60–61)
Operating since 1898, this
ferry ride is a "must do."

**Symphony of Lights
(▷ 62–63)** Stunning light
show in Victoria Harbour.

Temple Street (▷ 64)
Market stands selling
almost everything.

**Ten Thousand Buddhas
Temple (▷ 82–83)**
So named due to the
sheer number of Buddha
statues within.

**Tian Tan Buddha and
Lantau Island (▷ 98–
99)** Giant bronze Buddha
atop a mountain at Po Lin.

**University Museum and
Art Gallery (▷ 36–37)**
A hidden gem with a fine
collection of Chinese
antiquities.

Victoria Peak (▷ 38–39)
Take the tram to the top of
the Peak for amazing views.

**Waterfront Promenade
(▷ 65)** By night or day
some of the most stunning
cityscapes in the world.

**Wong Tai Sin Temple
(▷ 84)** Vast temple
complex with gardens.

These pages are a quick guide to the Top 25, which are described in more detail later. Here they are listed alphabetically and the tinted background shows the area they are in.

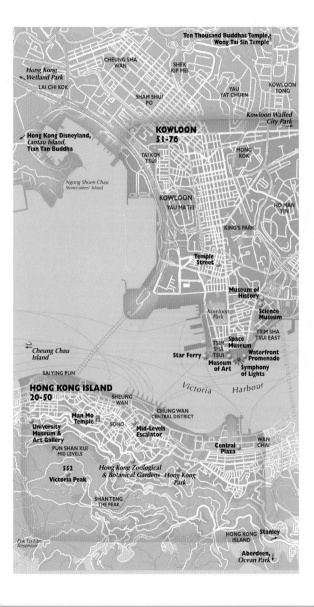

Ten Thousand Buddhas Temple,
Wong Tai Sin Temple

CHEUNG SHA WAN

SHEK KIP MEI

Hong Kong Wetland Park

LAI CHI KOK

YAU YAT CHUEN

KOWLOON TONG

SHAM SHUI PO

Kowloon Walled City Park

Hong Kong Disneyland, Lantau Island, Tian Tan Buddha

KOWLOON 51-76

TAI KOK TSUI

MONG KOK

Ngong Shuen Chau Stonecutters' Island

KOWLOON YAU MA TEI

HO MAN TIN

KING'S PARK

Temple Street

Museum of History

Cheung Chau Island

Kowloon Park

Science Museum

TSIM SHA TSUI EAST

Space Museum

SAI YING PUN

TSIM SHA TSUI

Waterfront Promenade

Star Ferry

HONG KONG ISLAND 20-50

SHEUNG WAN

CHUNG WAN CENTRAL DISTRICT

Museum of Art

Symphony of Lights

Victoria Harbour

Man Mo Temple

SOHO

Mid-Levels Escalator

WAN CHAI

University Museum & Art Gallery

PUN SHAN KUI MID LEVELS

Central Plaza

552 Victoria Peak

Hong Kong Zoological & Botanical Gardens

Hong Kong Park

SHAN TENG THE PEAK

Pok Fu Lam Reservoir

HONG KONG ISLAND

Stanley

Aberdeen, Ocean Park

Shopping

Hong Kong is a great place for shopping. Among locals it is a way of life rather than a trip to get necessities. The whole family will visit one of the shopping centers to enjoy the food halls, the air-conditioning and the experience of planning their next purchase. For visitors there are the many craft items to carry home as souvenirs, but another reason to shop in Hong Kong is that many items such as cameras, electronics, clothes, shoes and glasses can be cheaper here than in Europe. American visitors may pick up a few bargains, too, but if you want to buy something be aware of the price at home. Also, on large new items you may be charged import duties on your return home, and there is the inconvenience of getting things back damaged.

Emporia and Flea Markets

The most popular items with visitors are in the big Chinese emporia and flea markets. Look out for hand-embroidered silk shawls and blouses, Chinese slippers, all kinds of silk cushion covers and bedspreads. There are lots of tailors in Hong Kong who can make suits or shirts within a few days at relatively inexpensive prices. For bargain hunters there are many factory shops and outlets, where all kinds of seconds and end-of-run clothes are available

BARGAINING

Bargaining is an essential part of the shopping skills of the Hong Konger. They are of little use in department stores or other fixed-price establishments but in the markets or smaller shops bargaining is essential.

A good idea when bargaining is to know roughly how much the item costs in a fixed-price shop and aim to conclude the deal at a slightly lower price than that. Try a few practice bargains first to get the hang of it and be aware that, especially in highly touristy areas, the trader may assume you have no idea of the value of an item and ask for far too much in the hope that you'll fall for it.

From traditional Chinese products to international designer stores, Hong Kong has it all

at a fraction of the retail price. However, these places need some determined assessing and you should be prepared for bad days when there is little worth buying. Another serious contender for your vacation funds is jewelry, either made with semiprecious stones or cloisonné, or really expensive pieces made with diamonds and precious stones. Gold jewelry is beautifully made, often using Chinese characters as a design feature. Hong Kong is a great place to buy jade and the tourist board organizes an hour-long seminar on how to look for the best jade. Flea markets, such as at Cat Street (Upper Lascar Row), offer Mao memorabilia, posters, jewelry and much more.

Chinese Specialties

Ceramics are also an excellent purchase, with both Chinese and Western dinner services, teapots in handmade basket cozies and abstract pottery some of the best things to look out for. Chinese cooking utensils are inexpensive to buy in the wetmarkets and are very useful and visually interesting. Also attractive are bamboo steaming baskets for vegetables and tiffin carriers—stacked metal containers for carrying your lunch to work. Inexpensive and difficult to get outside of Chinese communities are Chinese dried goods and herbal remedies such as ginseng, dried fish such as abalone and shark's fin, and even birds' nests. Chinese tea is also a good buy. Kites and wooden toys are excellent, too, and there are crafts from other parts of Asia that are also reasonably priced.

SAFE SHOPPING

The Hong Kong Tourist Board has produced an excellent booklet called *A Guide to Quality Shops and Restaurants*, which lists all the places that have qualified under its scheme called QTS. The printed guide is a little heavy to carry around so, before you head off in search of a particular restaurant or supplier of goods, you can check members of the scheme at www.discoverhongkong.com.

Shopping by Theme

Whether you're looking for a department store, a quirky boutique, or something in between, you'll find it all in Hong Kong. On this page shops are listed by theme. For a more detailed write-up, see the individual listings in Hong Kong by Area.

ANTIQUES

Cat Street Galleries
(▷ 44)
Honeychurch Antiques
(▷ 44)
Karin Weber Antiques
(▷ 45)
Picture This (▷ 45)

ARTS AND CRAFTS

Chocolate Rain (▷ 44)
Mountain Folkcraft
(▷ 45)

CHINESE EMPORIA

Chinese Arts and Crafts
(HK) Ltd. (▷ 44, 70)
Yue Hwa Chinese
Products Emporium
(▷ 71)

COMPUTERS

Mong Kok Computer
Centre (▷ 71)
Windsor House Computer
Plaza (▷ 45)

ELECTRONICS

Broadway (▷ 70)
Fortress (▷ 70)

JEWELRY

Chow Tai Fook (▷ 44)
Elissa Cohen Jewellery
(▷ 70)
Just Gold (▷ 70)
Larry Jewelry (▷ 45)
Oriental Arts Jewelry
(▷ 71)
Tse Sui Luen Jewellery
(▷ 71)

MEN'S CLOTHES

Causeway Bay (▷ 44)
Sam's (▷ 71)
W. W. Chan & Sons
(▷ 45)

SHOPPING AREAS AND MALLS

Festival Walk (▷ 70)
Harbour City (▷ 70)
Lo Wu Commercial City
(▷ 106)

Ngong Ping Village
(▷ 106)
Pacific Place (▷ 45)
Rise Commercial Building
(▷ 71)
Sha Tin (▷ 89)
The Shoppes (▷ 106)

STREET MARKETS

Jardine's Crescent
(▷ 45)
Ladies' Market (▷ 71)
Li Yuen Street Market
(▷ 45)
Tai Po Market (▷ 89)
Upper Lascar Row
(Cat Street, ▷ 45)

WOMEN'S CLOTHES

G.O.D (▷ 44)
Granville Road (▷ 70)
Harbour City (▷ 70)

Hong Kong by Night

Hong Kong Island is the place to head for after-dark kicks. The dining and drinking district of Lan Kwai Fong (LKF) is the most obvious draw. It's a pedestrianized city block, full of buildings that house glitzy-but-expensive watering holes on lower floors. The bars tend to be popular with young professionals seeking refreshment after a day's money-making in front of the office monitor. Towards midnight, there's a fiesta atmosphere, with the party spilling out onto the street.

Relaxing

To the east, the district of Wan Chai was the base for sleazy clubs during the days of the Vietnam war. It is slightly more respectable now, with its hostess bars charging a fortune for a beer, but also some good clubs and bars. Wan Chai is home to some relaxed pubs if all you want is a quiet drink. With its wine bars, the Star Street precinct, between Wanchai and Admiralty, is good for those seeking greater refinement.

Party with the Locals

Kowloon also offers places to party, especially in touristy Tsim Sha Tsui (TST) where there are many bars and clubs around Knutsford Terrace, as well as places to go just for a drink. The bars generally open around midday and close after 2am, while clubs open from around 6pm and stay open until around 1am on weekdays and as late as 4am on the weekends.

There are plenty of bars, clubs and restaurants to try in Hong Kong

HOSTESS CLUBS

Hong Kong developed a racy reputation in the 1960s and 1970s when it became popular with American soldiers. Though sleaze is now fairly well hidden, there are some traces of Hong Kong's lurid side in the hostess clubs. These are mainly concentrated in TST and Wan Chai where customers may inadvertently find themselves on the wrong end of a huge bill. Be warned. Though advertised drink prices may sound reasonable, customers may be charged for merely talking to one of the scantily clad service staff.

Eating Out

Along with shopping, eating is another favorite pastime. Hong Kong has one of the highest per capita ratio of restaurants in the world. Although the city is famed for its Cantonese cuisine, it also has many international and fusion restaurants.

Cantonese Cuisine

Typical Cantonese dishes include crab in black bean sauce, steamed fish, shrimp with chili sauce, roast pigeon and fried noodles with beef. Meals are often accompanied by Chinese tea, the three basic types being green, black and oolong. Needless to say, milk and sugar aren't required.

Where to Eat

Restaurants in the more expensive hotels serve high quality cuisine, while restaurants on the outlying islands tend to specialize in sea-food. Street vendors, though no longer so prev-alent, sell a variety of reasonably priced snacks, such as fish balls, noodles and roast chestnuts. If you are feeling brave you can forgo the bigger places and try out your chopstick skills (▷ 50) in one of the tiny street cafés selling pork and rice or dim sum (▷ 48).

Opening Hours

Restaurants usually open for lunch around 11.30am, closing at 3pm and opening again for dinner between 6 and 11pm. A 10 percent service charge is often added to the bill in the smarter restaurants, while tips aren't expected in cheaper local restaurants.

AFTERNOON TEA

The red pillar boxes have all been repainted green, but the British ritual of afternoon tea is still going strong. For the full works in surroundings of sophistication and luxury, the lobby lounge at the InterContinental (▷ 112) is hard to beat, but the Grand Hyatt in Wan Chai (▷ 112) and the Mandarin Oriental (▷ 112) are worthy (and equally expensive) alternatives.

Hong Kongers love to eat and the island has both Cantonese and international restaurants choose from

Restaurants by Cuisine

There are restaurants to suit all tastes and budgets in Hong Kong. On this page they are listed by cuisine. For a more detailed description of each restaurant, see Hong Kong by Area.

Top Tips For…

However you'd like to spend your time in Hong Kong, these top suggestions should help you tailor your ideal visit. Each sight or listing has a fuller write-up elsewhere in the book.

ISLAND HOPPING

Spend a day at Cheung Chau (▷ 94) walking and lazing on the beach.
Get away from traffic on Lamma (▷ 100) with its seafood restaurants, bars and beaches.
Soar above Lantau (▷ 98) on the shiny Skyrail cable car and see the giant Buddha.
Take a trip out to tiny Po Toi (▷ 101) for challenging walks, great views and rock carvings.

PAMPERING

Soothe away all your stress with a mudbath and massage at the Four Seasons Spa (▷ 46).
Have an underwater massage at Chuan Spa (▷ 73) in Mong Kok.
Try the reflexology and aromatherapy, then have a sauna at the Island Shangri-La (▷ 112).
Spend your whole visit at the Plateau Spa accommodations at the Grand Hyatt (▷ 112).

Spa pampering (above) and retail therapy (below)

SHOPPING MALLS

Indulge in a little retail therapy at the Harbour City (▷ 70).
Wander for hours without seeing daylight in Pacific Place (▷ 45).
Cool down with an ice skate at the cavernous Festival Walk (▷ 70).

SKYSCRAPERS

Tell the time using the roof of Central Plaza (▷ 26).
Check out the inside-out Hong Kong & Shanghai Banking Corporation Building (▷ 41).
Wonder at the stylish 70-story Bank of China Tower (▷ 40) with its mixture of Ming dynasty and ultramodern design.

Skyscrapers of Central district (right)

Browsing the Stanley Market; Man Mo Temple (below)

MARKETS

Take the bus out to Stanley (▷ 34) where the market fills the town.

Refresh your wardrobe with inexpensive clothes at the Ladies' Market (▷ 71).

Bargain for antiques, Mao memorabilia and other kitsch curiosities and bric-a-brac at Upper Lascar Row (▷ 45).

Buy a piece of jade and try the seafood at Temple Street Night Market (▷ 64).

TEMPLES

Meet gods Man and Mo at the colorful Man Mo Temple (▷ 30).

Have your fortune told by a professional at the huge Wong Tai Sin Temple (▷ 84).

Count the Buddha statues at the Ten Thousand Buddhas Temple (▷ 82).

Visit one of the temples dedicated to Tin Hau, the goddess of seafarers. Try the one in Stanley (▷ 34).

PARTYING

Revel the night away in the Wan Chai's district's hedonistic bars and clubs (▷ 47).

Hang out with gweilos at Bahama Mama's (▷ 73).

Enjoy the after-work vibe at Staunton's (▷ 47).

Experience a cocktail with a view at stylish Sevva (▷ 47).

Hong Kong nightlife (above)

ROOMS WITH A VIEW

Request a room with a harbor view at the InterContinental (▷ 112).

Gaze down from one of Hong Kong's highest guestrooms in the Ritz-Carlton (▷ 112).

Peer over skyscraper roofs from the Island Shangri-La tower (▷ 112).

A luxurious harbor-view room at the Shangri-La (left)

STROLLS IN THE PARK

The Zoological and Botanical Gardens (below)

Check out the beautiful, but man-made, splendors of Hong Kong Park (▷ 27).
See trees, plants and animals from around the world at the Zoological and Botanical Gardens (▷ 28).
Admire the statue avenue, bird life and landscaped ponds of Kowloon Park (▷ 67).
Enjoy the remains of the notorious Kowloon Walled City in Kowloon Walled City Park (▷ 54).

USING CHOPSTICKS

Exercise your digits at the Jumbo Palace Floating Restaurant (▷ 49).
Grapple with street food at a *dai pai dong* (▷ panel, 49).
Seize some traditional Cantonese cuisine at Yung Kee Restaurant (▷ 50).

ENTERTAINING THE KIDS

See the pandas and enjoy the rides at Ocean Park (▷ 32).
Meet the leopards and orangutans at the Zoological Gardens (▷ 28).
Take a sampan ride round Aberdeen Harbour (▷ 24).
Get hands-on at the Hong Kong Science Museum (▷ 57).

WHAT'S FREE

Chinese bowl and chopsticks; a sea lion at Ocean Park (above)

Climb to the top of the Peak and admire the amazing views from Lugard Road (▷ 38).
Enjoy the exhibits at the University Museum and Art Gallery (▷ 36).
Goggle at the Symphony of Lights (▷ 62).
Ride the escalator to the Mid-Levels part of town (▷ 31).
Spend a day at Silverstrand beach (▷ 89).
View from the Peak (right)

Hong Kong by Area

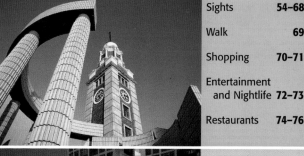

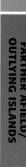

From shopping malls to sandy beaches, temples to theme parks, haute cuisine to dim sum, and designer labels to souvenirs, Hong Kong Island has it all.

Macau

Discovery Bay (Lantau Island)

Cheung Chau

Peng Chau,
Mui Wo

Yung Shue Wan,
So Kwu Wan (Lamma Island)

Ma Wan (Park Island)

SAI YING PUN

Hong Kong–Macau
Ferry Terminal

WESTERN HARBOUR CROSSING

Airport Express Line

Pier 2   Pier 3
Central   Pier 4   Pier 5
Ferry Piers

Man Kwong Street

Fung Mat Road

CONNAUGHT   ROAD   WEST

DES   VOEUX   ROAD   WEST

CONNAUGHT   ROAD

Western Fire
Services Street

New Market St

Sheung
Wan

**SHEUNG
WAN**

CENTRAL

Queen's Road West

First   Street
Centre Street
Second   Street
Third   Street

Sai   Street
Ying Pin

Hollywood
Park

Sheung Wan
Market

Queen's Road

Wing Lok St
Des Voeux Road Central

**Bonham
Strand**

Central
Market

International
Finance Centre

**Two
IFC**

BONHAM

ROAD

Hospital
Path

King George V
Memorial Park

BONHAM   PARK   ROAD

New   Road

Blake
Garden

**Man Mo
Temple**

Wing Kut St

SOHO

**Mid-
Levels
Escalator**

HONG KONG

**Exchange
Square**

Central

**University
Museum &
Art Gallery**

Pok Fu Lam Road

Bonham   Road

Hong Kong
University

Babington Path

Ulterton

Road

Museum
of Medical
Sciences

ROBINSON   ROAD

CAINE   ROAD

Ohel Leah Synagogue

Robinson   Road

Conduit   Road

**Hollywood
Road**

Lyndhurst Terrace

Wellington St

Graham St

Gage St

Queen's Rd Central

Lan Kwai Fong

D'Aguilar St

Wyndham St

**HSBC
Building**

Governmen
House

**PUN SHAN KUI
MID LEVELS**

**Dr Sun Yat-sen
Museum**

**Jamia
Masjid**

UPPER ALBERT ROAD

**PEAK TRAM
TERMINAL**

Garden
Road

University   Drive

Kotewall   Road

Conduit   Road

Po   Shan   Road

Po Shan Road

Lugard   Road

**Hong Kong Zoological
& Botanical Gardens**

Kennedy
Road

Harlech   Road

Mt Austin   Road

552

Victoria Peak

Victoria
Peak
Garden

The Governor's Walk

Hammer   Path

Old   Peak   Road

MacDonnell Road

Macdonnell
Road

May   Road

May
Road

Chatham   Path

Peak Tramway

**493
▲ Sai Ko Shan
High West**

Harlech   Road

Findlay   Road

**Peak
Tower**

**SHAN TENG
THE PEAK**

Barker
Road

Barker   Road

Hospital Path

Lugard   Road

*Pok Fu Lam
Country Park*

250 m

250 yds

Pok Fu Lam Reservoir Road

Pok Fu Lam Reservoir Road

Peak   Road

Plantation   Road

Severn   Road

Coombe   Road

Gough Hill   Road

Severn
Road

A   **B**   **C**

Tsim Sha Tsui East
Ferry Pier

New Hung Hom
Ferry Pier

Victoria   *Harbour*

New Hung Hom
Ferry Pier,
Sai Wan Ho

Pier 8
Hong Kong Maritime Museum
Pier 9

**CHUNG WAN
NTRAL DISTRICT**

Wan Chai
Ferry Pier

**Hong Kong
Convention and
Exhibition Centre**

Convention Avenue

Hung Hing Road

**WAN
CHAI**

City Hall

Lung Wo   Road

Central
Government
Offices

Harbour Road

Statue
Square

Hong Kong Academy
for Performing Arts
HARCOURT ROAD

**Central
Plaza**

Harbour

P

Chater
Garden

**Bank of
China
Tower**

Admiralty

Drake Street

Harcourt
Garden

QUEENSWAY

ARSENAL ST

GLOUCESTER

ROAD

**Causeway
Bay**

John's
thedral

Museum of
Tea Ware

Jaffe Road

HENNESSY   ROAD

Lockhart Road

HENNESSY   ROAD

Thomson Road

Wan Chai

**Aberdeen,
Ocean Park**

**Hong Kong
Park**

QUEEN'S   ROAD

JOHNSTON   ROAD

Thomson Road

QUEEN'S ROAD EAST

Sikh
Temple

Muslim
Cemetery

Bowen Road

Kennedy Road

Tai Wong
Temple

Kennedy Road

Hong Kong
Cemetery

STUBBS

GAP

ROAD

PEAK

ROAD

Tai Wong

**Pak Tai
Temple**

Shiu Fai Terrace

Bowen   Road

Black's Link

ROAD

STUBBS

**Repulse Bay,
Stanley**

Police
Museum

P

Wan
Chai Gap

**HONG KONG
ISLAND**

Mount Nicholson Road

Magazine Gap Road

Middle Gap Road

E   F

Aberdeen

JUMBO FLOATING RESTAURANT

HIGHLIGHTS

● Dinner at the Jumbo Floating Restaurant (▷ 49)
● A sampan ride around the harbor
● Views over the harbor from the Chinese cemetery above the town

TIP

● Ap Lei Chau has become a hot spot of outlets where anything from last year's designer clothing at knock-down prices, to furniture and antiques can be found.

Before the British arrived, Aberdeen was a small fishing village, full of pirates and smugglers. Today the pirates are gone, but fishing remains the livelihood of many families.

Fragrant Harbor Aberdeen is known in Chinese as Heung Gong Tsai, meaning "little fragrant harbor"; this name is thought to have derived from the village's trade in sandalwood and incense production. The whole of the Special Administrative Region (SAR) is now described by this term, Hong Kong. The chief draw of a visit to Aberdeen, which is actually the second largest urban area in the SAR, is to visit the harbor, where for centuries families have lived their lives on houseboats all moored tightly together. At the western end of the harbor is the wholesale fish market.

Aberdeen harbor is full of life, being home to a large fishing fleet and hundreds of people living on junks. It is renowned for its floating restaurants, of which the most famous is the Jumbo Floating Restaurant–with a staff of more than 300

Highlights A highlight of your visit is to negotiate with one of the savvy old ladies that ply tourists around the harbor. Take a trip out to Ap Lei Chau (around HK$50), a tiny island just offshore (either by junk or via the more mundane road that links the island with Aberdeen). The 28-floor Horizon Plaza, on Lee Wing Street, is great for discounted fashions and reproductions. Back in Aberdeen, the Tin Hau Temple in Reservoir Road, dedicated to the goddess of the sea, is worth a look, followed by a walk uphill to the huge cemetery with views over the harbor.

Floating restaurants There are two mega-restaurants in Aberdeen harbor catering to the vast numbers of people who come out here to eat the seafood as a tourist experience. Free ferries take customers out to the restaurants.

THE BASICS

✚ See map ▷ 92–93
✉ Aberdeen
🍴 The two floating restaurants of Jumbo Kingdom, bars and cafés in town
🚌 70 from Exchange Square
🚇 MTR (opens in 2015)
♿ Few
🚤 Sampan boats: inexpensive

Central Plaza

TOP
25

Views of Central Plaza in Wan Chai

THE BASICS

www.centralplaza.com.hk

🔹 F10

✉ 18 Harbour Road, Wan Chai

☎ 2586 8111

🍴 Nearby cafés

🚇 Wan Chai

♿ Good

🎟 Free

HIGHLIGHTS

● Brooding neoclassical grandeur of interior
● Artwork in the lobby
● Quiet spot in forecourt outside the building
● Views from the 46th floor

Completed in 1992, Central Plaza was, for a few years, Hong Kong's tallest building. It rises to 78 floors and stands at 1,227ft (374m)—counting the spire.

Majestic It's not often an office block is included in a list of tourist destinations, but this one certainly deserves a visit for its stunning architecture and for the views from the observation point on the 46th floor. Confusingly located in Wan Chai (you'd think it would be in Central with a name like that), the building looks from a distance like a huge glass prism with its triangular shape and acres of plate glass. The top of the reinforced concrete building forms a clock with four different color neon panels changing their configuration every 15 minutes. Considered by some to be overdecorated, the sheer glass walls include the design, in gold, of the outline of a smaller building. Downstairs at ground level is a tiny garden, which is good for a quiet moment in the surrounding urban chaos. From here an escalator leads up to the wide public piazza filled with exotic plants that forms a public access bridge across Wan Chai.

Highest church The building was actually meant to be taller than it is but an economic downturn during its construction led to a reduction in height. It is no longer one of the ten tallest buildings in China, but Central Plaza is blessed by being the home of the highest church in the world: it sits on the top office floor below the huge glass atrium.

Plants and birds in the aviary at Hong Kong Park

Hong Kong Park

In a space-deprived Hong Kong, this modern park is a joy. Instead of roses or ancient trees you'll find man-made waterfalls, concrete pools and paths around the grass and flowers, providing a sense of harmony and balance.

Artificial paradise Hong Kong Park is a miracle of artificiality. Its architects used what little original landscape existed and built the park into the contours of the hillside. It's fun to walk past the pools filled with koi carp or through the Edward Youde Aviary where tree-high walkways take you cheek-by-bill with brightly plumaged tropical birds.

The conservatory The Forsgate conservatory is a huge building. It has three separate sections—display plants, humid plants and dry plants—which take up a large chunk of the entire park. Adjustable climate control equipment simulates conditions from disparate regions. The varieties of bamboo are particularly impressive.

Refreshments old and new The Museum of Teaware in Flagstaff House, the oldest colonial building in Hong Kong, deserves a look. Flagstaff House is a charming piece of mid-19th century architecture, and the exhibition of teapots and the like brings out the collector in almost everyone. Most afternoons the park is full of elegantly dressed parties posing for wedding photos, having just emerged from the registry office, which is in the park.

THE BASICS

www.lcsd.gov.hk/parks/hkp

🔲 D11

✉ Main entrance: Supreme Court Road, Central. Nearest entrance to Museum of Teaware: Cotton Tree Drive, Central

☎ Museum: 2869 0690

🕐 Park: 6am–11pm. Museum: Wed–Mon 10–5. Aviary and Conservatory 9am–5pm. Closed 24–25 Dec, 1 Jan, and first 3 days of Chinese New Year

🍴 Café/bar in park

🚇 Admiralty

🚌 12, 23B, 40, 103; get off at first stop in Cotton Tree Drive

♿ Good 🖐 Free

HIGHLIGHTS

● Walk-in aviary
● Artificial waterfalls
● Conservatory
● Flagstaff House and Museum of Teaware
● Observation tower
● Bonsai trees in t'ai chi garden

Hong Kong Zoological and Botanical Gardens

- Bromeliads, air plants and carnivorous plants
- Amazing variety of butterflies, especially in fall
- Jaguar
- Orangutan families
- Tree kangaroos from central New Guinea
- Flamingos

In the middle of the urban sprawl these gardens form a quiet haven of peace. In fall, the scent of flowers fills the air and the wings of myriad butterflies shimmer in the light with a dazzling color.

Oasis of calm This century-old complex, which once looked out over Victoria Harbour, is enclosed today by the city's towers (and bisected by a road; use the underpass to get from one part to the other). There are 300 species of birds, including many rare ones that breed happily in captivity. In the greenhouse are air plants, bromeliads and insectivorous plants such as pitcher plants, Venus fly-traps and rare butterworts. Early in the morning the gardens are full of people performing the slow exercise program known as t'ai chi ch'uan, which is

There are more than 1,000 plant species in the Botanical Gardens, while the zoo has successfully bred endangered species, such as the ring-tailed lemur (far left)

designed to get the life forces flowing properly around the body. The zoo, though small, is surprisingly comprehensive and has a number of endangered species. The zoo specializes in primates and has orangutans from Sabah and lion-tailed macaque from India.

Government House Opposite the gardens is Government House, where Hong Kong's British governors used to live. The house was built in 1855 and was added to through the years, perhaps one of the most attractive additions being the Japanese tower and roof corners that were put up during the Occupation. Government House, official residence of Hong Kong's Chief Executive, is closed to the public, but you can peer through the gates or visit its pretty gardens when they open for two days in March.

THE BASICS

www.lcsd.gov.hk/parks

✚ C10

✉ Several entrances; from Central the most accessible gate is on Upper Albert Road

☎ 2530 0154

🕓 Gardens, zoo, aviaries: daily 6am–7pm (Fountain terrace garden 5am–10pm). Greenhouses: 9–4.30

🚇 Central

🚌 3B, 12, 13 from Central; 12A, 12M, 40, 40M, 40P from Admiralty

🍴 Snack kiosk

♿ Good

🎟 Free

Man Mo Temple

TOP 25

The altar (below left) and Man Mo incense coils (below)

THE BASICS

www.lcsd.gov.hk/CE/Museum/Monument

✚ C9

✉ 124–126 Hollywood Road (near Ladder Street)

🕐 Daily 8–6

🚇 Sheung Wan

🚌 26

♿ Access difficult

🎟 Free

HIGHLIGHTS

● Statues of Man Cheong and Kuan Ti
● Sedan chairs once used to carry the statues
● Embroideries surrounding the statues
● Drum and bell on right of entrance door
● Soot-blackened deities on left of entrance door
● Gold and brass standards carried during parades
● Resident fortune-tellers

The most remarkable aspect of this tiny, but historic, temple is the canopy of incense coils which create a heady, mysterious atmosphere.

Taoism The temple, built in 1847, is one of the oldest surviving structures on Hong Kong Island and looks rather bullied by the soaring apartment blocks that surround it. It is dedicated to two Taoist deities who represent the pen and the sword. These are Man, or Man Cheong, the god of literature; and Mo, or Kuan Ti, the god of war. The statues of Man and Mo are dressed lavishly in beautifully embroidered outfits. Beside the two main statues in the temple are representations of Pao Kung, the god of justice, and Shing Wong, the god who protects this region of the city. By the door are the figures of some lesser deities. A drum and a gong are sounded whenever an offering is made to the gods. The atmosphere seems casual—cats wander around, fortune-tellers divine the future using *chim* (numbered bamboo sticks), and visitors place offerings of fruit or incense sticks in the offering boxes next to the statues inside the temple.

Nearby sights Next door, to the right, is the Lit Shing Kung, or All Saints Temple. Here, too, you can see people consulting resident soothsayers, who interpret the *chim* tipped out of bamboo pots. In the courtyard of the temple stand gilded plaques, carried in processions, while inside are the two 1862 sedan chairs used to convey the figures of the two gods.

Mid-Levels Escalator

The world's longest outdoor escalator system runs to 2,625ft (800m), comprising 20 distinct sections.

Up It was built in the early 1990s to ease traffic congestion in the narrow streets below but has had the effect of breathing new life into whole swathes of Central, not least the wining and dining district of SoHo. Used by around 54,000 pedestrians each day, it operates downhill until 10am and uphill thereafter, easing the commute for the salarymen and women who live in the upmarket Mid-Levels district.

Down The escalator starts at 100 Queen's Road Central, emerging from next to the Central Market building. This 1930s Bauhaus building sits on the site of Hong Kong's oldest colonial market, established in 1842. The route then takes walkers up Cochrane Street, across Hollywood Road to Shelley Street and then on to Conduit Road, high in the Mid-Levels.

All around Notable streets en route include Hollywood Road, a haven for collectors of art and antiques. There's a great view from here of the imposing Central Police Station, built between 1841 and 1925. It's worth descending here and heading to Graham Street and one of Hong Kong's best outdoor markets. The streets beyond Hollywood Road, commonly known as SoHo, have been reborn as a drinking and dining hub thanks to the elevator. Beyond, near the top of the escalator, is the Jamia Mosque.

THE BASICS

- C10
- 100 Queens Road Central, Central
- Daily 6am–midnight
- Gage Street, Staunton Street
- Central
- Poor

HIGHLIGHTS

- Central Market building
- Gage Street
- Graham Street
- Central Police Station
- SoHo
- Jamia Mosque

Ocean Park

HIGHLIGHTS

● The Grand Aquarium
● Ocean Theatre animal shows
● Raging River flume ride
● Le Le and Ying Ying
● Emperors of the Sky bird show
● Dragon Ride and Hair Raiser

TIPS

● Avoid the weekends when things get very crowded.
● The cable car ride may be closed down in inclement weather.

Wildlife, history, scenic views, arts and crafts, and animal shows—not to mention thrilling rides—make up this park. It's a whole day's entertainment—and a jam-packed day at that.

Thrills galore There is so much to see and do at this park that it takes a little time to plan your visit. Find out the times and locations of the animal shows and organize your day around them.

Aerial view The park is divided into two main sections with rollercoasters and animal attractions divided roughly equally. The lowland section is called The Waterfront, while the upland section is The Summit. Transit between them is by either the funicular Thrill Mountain, or, best of all, the cable car which has views over the park and sea.

What to See Ocean Park's first giant pandas—An An and Jia Jia—occupy the Hong Kong Jockey Club Sichuan Treasures attraction. The younger pandas—Le Le and Ying Ying—arrived as babies in 2007 and can be found in the Giant Panda Adventure. The Grand Aquarium encourages kids to touch some of the friendlier creatures, and has a multi-level walk-through tank. At the summit is Marine World, home to the jellyfish and shark exhibits, the Ocean Theatre, and the Ocean Park Tower, which rotates passengers at a height of 236ft (72m) for spectacular views.

Rides Both areas have rides, though younger children will prefer the Whiskers Harbour zone in the park's Waterfront section. At The Summit sits the Dragon, the Hair Raiser and the Abyss roller-coasters, each stomach-churning in their own way.

THE BASICS

www.oceanpark.com.hk
✚ See map ▷ 92–93
✉ Ocean Park Road, Aberdeen
☎ 3923 2323
🕐 Daily 10–6
🍴 Fast-food, Bayview Restaurant Terrace Café
🚌 Citibus 629 leaves from Admiralty MTR every 10 min and leaves the Star Ferry Terminal every 20–60 min
♿ Excellent
💲 Expensive
❓ Height restrictions on some rides

Stanley

HIGHLIGHTS

● Views from bus to Stanley
● Tin Hau Temple
● Stanley Beach
● St. Stephen's Beach
● Stanley Military Cemetery
● Stanley Market
● Kuan Yin Temple

TIPS

● A 15-minute walk along Wong Ma Kok Road is a signpost down to the much nicer St. Stephen's Beach.
● Check out the Correctional Services Museum at 45 Tung Tau Wan Road (Tue–Sun 10–5). Admission is free.

The most stunning thing about a visit to Stanley, in the south of Hong Kong Island, is the journey there. Get an upstairs seat on the double-decker bus—the ride is as good as any at Ocean Park.

Temples Most visitors come to Stanley for its market, but the village has many other attractions. Close to the market is the Tin Hau Temple, first built on this spot in the early 1700s. The bell and drum are said to have belonged to a famous pirate, Cheung Po-Tsai. The bell was cast in 1767, and it is thought that the pirate used it to send messages to his ships. The temple also contains the skin of a tiger, shot in Stanley in 1942. Farther along the road is a second temple, dedicated to Kuan Yin, goddess of mercy. Some claim to have seen the 20ft (6m) statue of the goddess move.

Visit Stanley for its market, beaches and temples, or just for a walk along the seafront

Beaches and the market The beach at Stanley is a good one, and a short bus ride farther along takes you to St. Stephen's Beach, where there is a graveyard for all the soldiers who have died in Hong Kong since Britain claimed the island as a colony. Although now rather touristy, the famous market is quite good, with linen shops as well as stands selling clothes made in other Asian countries. Stanley is the stepping-off point for Po Toi Island (▷ 101), an hour's ferry ride away, but worth the trip for the prehistoric rock carvings and a good beach for swimming.

Stanley is also an increasingly popular diving destination. The three-story Murray House was relocated, stone-by-stone, from Central, where it was formerly a British Army barracks dating to 1848. It houses several restaurants, replete with verandas and terraces with sea views.

THE BASICS

➕ See map ▷ 92–93
🕐 Market: 10.30–6.30.
Temple: 6–6
🍴 Restaurants and pub food in Stanley Main Street
🚌 6, 6A, 6X, 66, 260 from Exchange Square
⛴ Ferries to Po Toi depart Sat 1.20, Sun 10, 11.30, 3.30 and 5
♿ Excellent

University Museum and Art Gallery

TOP 25

HIGHLIGHTS

- Nestorian bronze crosses
- Bronze mirrors
- Neolithic black pottery cup
- Pottery horse, Western Han dynasty
- Qing dynasty woodcarving
- Bronze drum
- Sui dynasty spittoons
- Indian Buddhist sculptures
- Modern Chinese pottery from Jinghdezhen and Shiwan

TIP

- The Tea Gallery serves tea in the traditional style: Mon–Sat 10–5, Sun 2–5.

This interesting collection of pre-dominantly Chinese objects is worth the effort to see it. The museum is on the University of Hong Kong campus and is usually blessedly empty.

Nestorian bronze crosses The exhibits in this out-of-the-way museum, in the university's Fung Ping Shan Building, date from the 5th century BC onward, but the highlight is a set of 467 Nestorian bronze crosses—the largest such collection in the world—which belonged to a Christian sect that originated in Syria and came to China during the Tang dynasty (AD618–906). The crosses date back to the Yuan dynasty (1280–1367) and were probably worn as part of a belt or as a pendant. They were made in various cross-shapes, including swastikas, birds and conventional crucifixes.

Since its foundation in 1953, the University Museum has amassed over 1,000 Chinese antiquities including bronze rice sculptures, a globe and wooden shutters (below)

Ceramics and bronzes Notable among the other bronze items on display are mirrors from the Warring States period (475–221BC), and Shang and Zhou ritual vessels and weapons. The museum also houses an enormous collection of ceramics dating back as far as neolithic times. The neolithic pottery is very fine, and the Han dynasty horse is full of life. Look for the three-color glaze Tang pottery, the famous kiln wares from the Song dynasty and the polychrome ceramics from the Ming and Qing dynasties.

Beyond Hong Kong Objects from other Asian countries include some Indian Buddhist sculptures and items from Thailand, Vietnam and Korea. Scroll paintings, inlaid blackwood furniture and a huge bronze drum make up the rest of the collection.

THE BASICS

www.hku.hk/hkumag
+ A9
✉ 90 Bonham Road
☎ 2241 5500
🕐 Mon–Sat 9.30–6, Sun 1–6. Closed public holidays
🚇 Sheung Wan
🚌 3B from City Hall on Connaught Road or 23, 40, 40M from Pacific Place, Admiralty
♿ None
🎟 Free

Victoria Peak

HIGHLIGHTS

● Views over Hong Kong
● Tram ride to the top
● Old Governor's Lodge, with toposcope in its gardens
● Souvenirs in Peak Galleria
● Circular walk around Lugard and Harlech roads
● Green-arrowed walk up Mount Austin Road

TIPS

● If you can, make your trip to the Peak on a clear day.
● Take a picnic and do the walk around the Peak.

Visiting the Peak is one of the first things to do when you get to Hong Kong. At 1,811ft (552m) the hilltop views are spectacular and the area offers some peaceful, shady walks.

Head for heights Some people like to make the pilgrimage up the Peak twice—once during the day and again at night to see the city lights. Both are worthwhile, but Hong Kong's regular haze makes a night-time visit the safest bet if time is short. The Peak is a relatively unspoiled oasis in a concrete jungle, and a good place for a quiet walk.

Top stop The Peak Tower offers multiple distractions, including a Madame Tussauds and heaps of touristy shops. The highlight is the Sky Terrace 428, a ticketed 360-degree viewing

The best thing about the Peak is its breathtaking views over the city. Visit both during the day and after dark. The Peak Tower (bottom middle) was designed by British architect Terry Farrell in the shape of an upheld rice bowl

platform which boasts a spectacular view over Central, the harbor and Kowloon beyond. If you don't want to pay, the circular walk around the peak via Lugard and Harlech roads offers arguably even better views and will take less than an hour. Across the square from the Peak Tower is the Peak Galleria with its simple terrace and many restaurants and shops.

View from the top The trip up in the Peak Tram, constructed in 1888, is good fun as long as you don't have to line up for hours—avoid weekends and the first day after a misty spell. From the tram stop you can walk along Mount Austin Road to Victoria Park Gardens and the ruins of the Governor's Lodge, destroyed by the Japanese in World War II. A noticeboard outside the Peak Tower displays the hour-long walk routes.

THE BASICS

www.thepeak.com.hk

⊞ B11

✉ Peak Tower, Peak Road

🕐 Peak Tram: runs 7am–midnight

🍴 Cafés and restaurants

🚋 Trams run every 10–15 min from terminals at Garden Road and Cotton Tree Drive. Route 15 from Exchange Square

♿ Good

💲 Tram fare: moderate. Sky Terrace 428: moderate. Peak Tower: free

More to See

BANK OF CHINA TOWER

Designed by the Chinese-American architect I. M. Pei, and built between 1985 and 1990, this 1,205-ft (367m) high, 70-floor tower stands out amid the Hong Kong skyline. The building soars upward in a series of triangles toward a prism at the top. There is a 43rd-floor viewing platform (free), open Monday to Saturday.

🚇 D10 ✉ No. 1 Garden Road, Central ⏰ Mon–Fri 8–6 🚇 Central 🎫 Free

BONHAM STRAND

Ginseng shops, antiques markets and tiny lanes with ancient shops now abound on the road where the British first set foot. Despite the renovations this area still recalls the old Hong Kong and many of the old ways persist.

🚇 C9 ✉ Bonham Strand, Sheung Wan ⏰ Shops close on public holidays, Chinese New Year 🍴 Food stalls in Sheung Wan Market and streets around Bonham Strand; fast food near MTR station 🚇 Sheung Wan 🚋 Trams stop at Western Market and go on through Central to Causeway Bay 🅿 Good 🎫 Free

CAUSEWAY BAY

This district is famous for youth chic and rowdy local restaurants. It's particularly fun at night. It's home to the excellent Central Library as well as Happy Valley Racecourse.

🚇 H9 🍴 Many 🚇 Causeway Bay 🅿 Good

CHATER GARDEN

Chater Garden is a slice of tropical repose amid the bustling city. Once the site of the Hong Kong Cricket Club and its manicured lawn, it is surrounded by a clutch of Central's most iconic skyscrapers—the Bank of China Tower among them. Near by is Hong Kong's Cenotaph.

🚇 D10 ✉ Between Chater Road and Des Voeux Road ⏰ 24 hours 🚇 Central 🅿 Good

DR. SUN YAT-SEN MUSEUM

http://hk.drsunyatsen.museum

The arrival of a Sun Yat-Sen museum in Hong Kong feels like confirmation that Hong Kong is back in mainland hands. The

Early morning t'ai chi in Victoria Park, Causeway Bay

revered nationalist leader has museums dedicated to him in many major Chinese cities, but this one, in the 1914 Kom Tong Hall, really stands out, both in terms of the architecture, and its two excellent permanent exhibitions.

🔒 C10 ✉ 7 Castle Road, Mid Levels, Central ☎ 2367 6373 🕐 Mon–Wed and Fri–Sat 10–6, Sun 10–7 🚌 3B, 12, 23, 40 to Caine 🎫 Inexpensive

EXCHANGE SQUARE

Bounded by three ultramodern tower blocks, including the Hong Kong Stock Exchange, the square is linked via a series of overhead walkways to the Sheung Wan district. On Sundays, and without the hustle and bustle of weekday commerce, it is a place of quiet contemplation.

🔒 D9 🍴 Café and fast-food outlets 🚇 Exchange Square, Central 🦽 Good

HOLLYWOOD ROAD

If you are a serious antiques collector or just like browsing among junk and curios, then head to Hollywood Road. The antiques shops start at the beginning of the road and continue for about 1 mile (1.6km), incorporating Upper Lascar Row (▷ 45). Antiques that are more than 100 years old must have a certificate of authenticity. If you plan on spending a lot, you might want to check with your consulate first to find out if there will be duty charges. The importation and exportation of raw or worked ivory is governed by strict rules. It's best to check with customs officials to find out what paperwork is required to export ivory.

🔒 C10 🚇 Sheung Wan 🦽 Poor

HONG KONG CONVENTION & EXHIBITION CENTRE (HKCEC)

www.hkcec.com

The once-bland Convention & Exhibition Centre, originally built in 1988 on reclaimed land, underwent extensive expansion in 1997. The new structure has made an iconic impact on the Island's waterfront, being easily identified as the gargantuan spaceship-like building protruding into the harbor. The linked towers of the HKCEC contain two of the Island's most prestigious hotels—the Grand Hyatt (▷ 112) and the Renaissance Harbour View.

The adjacent Reunifiation Monument attracts many visitors.

🔒 F10 ✉ 1 Convention Avenue, Wan Chai ☎ 2582 8888 🚇 Wan Chai 🎫 Free

HONG KONG & SHANGHAI BANKING CORPORATION (HSBC) BUILDING

This 1985 building, designed by British architect Sir Norman Foster and prefabricated in several continents at a cost of over US$1 billion,

The Bank of China Tower

looks as if it's been turned inside out. The supporting structures appear on the outside, all mechanical parts are exposed, and many walls are glass. There is good public access to the impressive main lobby.

➕ D10 ✉ Des Voeux Road/Statue Square, Central 🚇 Central 💵 Free

REPULSE BAY
The pretty beach gets very crowded on public holidays and on the weekends, but is worth the trip. There is a temple and a modern shopping arcade here too.

➕ See map ▷ 92–93 🚌 6, 61 from Central Bus Terminus

ST. JOHN'S CATHEDRAL
This Anglican church, a relic of British colonialism, has stood since 1849. The dominant feature inside is the stained-glass representation of the crucifixion. The church can be found below the Lower Peak tram terminal on Garden Road.

➕ D10 ✉ 4-8 Garden Road ☎ 2523 4157 🕐 7–6 🚇 Central ♿ None

STATUE SQUARE
The highlight of this historic square is the neo-classical former Legislative Council (Legco) Building. Built in 1912, it now houses Hong Kong's Court of Final Appeal.

➕ D10 ✉ Between Chater Road and Des Voeux Road Central 🕐 24 hours 🚇 Central ♿ Excellent 💵 Free

TWO IFC
www.hkma.gov.hk
Two IFC is a monument to Hong Kong's post-colonial prosperity. Designed by Cesar Pelli, it rises to 1,362-ft (415m) spread over "88" floors. Eight is a lucky number across China, and "double eight" more so— Hong Kong Monetary Authority's chief executive has an office on 88th floor. Public access is limited, but there's a public museum on the 55th floor with great city views. Downstairs is a luxury mall and the Airport Express train occupies the basement.

➕ D9 ✉ 1 Harbour View Street, Central
HKMA Info Centre ☎ 2878 1111
🕐 Mon–Fri 10–6, Sat 10–1 💵 Free

The pretty beach at Repulse Bay

A statue of Sir Thomas Jackson Bart in Statue Square

An Island Walk

This inner city walk passes shops selling all manner of herbal remedies, then continues along famous Hollywood Road to Soho.

DISTANCE: 1.6 miles (2.5km) **ALLOW:** 1.5 hours

START

SHEUNG WAN MTR
➕ C9 🚇 Sheung Wan

END

LI YUEN STREETS EAST AND WEST
(▷ 45) ➕ C10 🚇 Central

① Start the walk at Sheung Wan MTR station and turn right outside Exit B on Des Voeux Road. Head toward the large Edwardian building of Western Market.

② Head south and turn right at a compasslike piazza on to Wing Lok Street. Tour the traditional Chinese shops selling ginseng, bird's nests and other dried ingredients. Return along Bonham Strand West before heading uphill and turning left on to Hollywood Road (▷ 41).

③ After a few bends and the many antiques, curios and jade shops take a left on Lok Ku Road and an immediate right onto the pedestrian route of Upper Lascar Row (Cat Street, ▷ 45).

④ At the end of this souvenir run turn right up the steps of Ladder Street to arrive at Man Mo Temple (▷ 30).

⑧ Finally turn right along Stanley Street to head east until Pottinger Street. The walk ends with the narrow market alleys of Pottinger Street and Li Yuen streets East and West (▷ 45).

⑦ Head downhill across Hollywood Road. Venture down from the escalator corridors to explore the small restaurants of Gage Street and the shops of Lyndhurst Terrace, returning to Cochrane Street below the escalator each time.

⑥ At the Mid-Levels escalator turn right if in need of the SoHo bars and restaurants, otherwise ascend to the escalator's bridges.

⑤ On leaving the temple turn right and continue for some 436 yards (400m) down Hollywood Road.

HONG KONG ISLAND WALK

Shopping

CAT STREET GALLERIES

This shopping complex full of antiques dealers and curio shops is close to the Hollywood Road antiques area.

🔼 B9 ⊠ 38 Lok Ku Road, Sheung Wan ☎ 2291 0006 🕐 Mon–Sat 11–7 🚇 Sheung Wan

CAUSEWAY BAY

This is a major shopping district but less touristy than Central or Tsim Sha Tsui. The huge Times Square mall is the centrepiece, housing, amongst others, Marks and Spencer and a large Lane Crawford store. You'll find a number of designer outlets in the Sogo and Hysan Place malls, while youth couture is well served in the many boutiques within the upscale Island Beverley Centre.

🔼 G10 🚇 Causeway Bay

CHINESE ARTS AND CRAFTS (HK) LTD.

www.cachk.com
Compared to other Chinese emporia, this one stocks more designer rosewood and lacquer furniture, lamps and carpets. You can find some pretty valuable pieces here. There are three other outlets in Central, Admiralty and TST.

🔼 F10 ⊠ 2/F, Causeway Centre, 28 Harbour Road, Wan Chai ☎ 2827 6667 🕐 Daily 10.30–7.30 🚇 Wan Chai

CHOCOLATE RAIN

www.chocolaterain.com
Chocolate Rain sells hand-made patchwork bags, dolls and jewelry—many pieces have a cutesy chic borrowed from Japanese pop culture. Souvenirs for the fashionably minded.

🔼 C10 ⊠ 1/F, PMQ, 35 Aberdeen Street, Central ☎ 2559 0017 🕐 Daily 12–9 🚇 Central

CHOW TAI FOOK

www.chawtaifook.com
This is just one of a good local jewelry chain that has branches in Causeway Bay, Central and around Mong Kok. Checkout the jade and watch the way local people go about the serious business of buying.

🔼 C10 ⊠ G2 Aon China

Building, 29 Queen's Road, Central ☎ 2523 7128 🕐 Daily 10–8:30 🚇 Central

G.O.D.

www.god.com.hk
The initials of this Hong Kong boutique stand for "Goods of Desire". It's self-consciously chic, with something to please every taste, from fashions to furniture, music to greetings cards. There are seven more locations dotted around the city.

🔼 C10 ⊠ 48 Hollyood Road, Central ☎ 2523 5561 🕐 Mon–Sat 10.30–7, Sun 12.30–7 🚇 Central

HONEYCHURCH ANTIQUES

www.honeychurch.com
Browse here for antique silverware, utensils and jewelry, as well as ornaments and items from around the world.

🔼 C10 ⊠ 29 Hollywood Road, Central ☎ 2543 2433 🕐 Mon–Sat 10–6 🚇 Central

ISLAND BEVERLY CENTRE

This treasure trove of youth fashion is well hidden amid the neon splatter in Causeway Bay. Contained within are row after row of small stores and boutiques selling local, Japanese and Korean couture. One for the kids.

🔼 H10 ⊠ 1 Great George Street, Causeway Bay ☎ 2890 6823 🕐 Daily noon–11pm 🚇 Causeway Bay

JARDINE'S CRESCENT

Crowds flock to this little lane for imitation fashions at a medley of trendy boutiques. The place really comes alive at night.
🔲 H10 ✉ Jardine's Crescent, Causeway Bay ⏰ Daily mid-morning to late 🚇 Causeway Bay

KARIN WEBER ANTIQUES

www.karinwebergallery.com
Here you'll find a mixture of arts and crafts, modern Asian pieces and Chinese country antiques.
🔲 C10 ✉ Ground floor 20 Aberdeen Street, Central ☎ 2544 5004 ⏰ Mon–Sat 11–7, Sun 1–6 🚇 Central

LARRY JEWELRY

www.larryjewelry.com
One of several branches of the internationally famous jeweler.
🔲 C10 ✉ G/F, 72 Queen's Road Central, Central ☎ 2521 1268 ⏰ Daily 10–7 🚇 Central

LI YUEN STREET MARKET

A clothes, handbag, fabric and accessories market, one of Hong Kong's oldest, where you'll find excellent bargains.
🔲 C10 ✉ Off Queen's Road Central, Central ⏰ Daily 12–late 🚇 Central

MOUNTAIN FOLKCRAFT

www.mountainfolkcraft.com
Delightful handmade paintings, carvings and *batik* from Southeast Asia.
🔲 C10 ✉ 12 Wo On Lane, Central ☎ 2523 2817 ⏰ Mon–Sat 10–6.30 🚇 Central

PACIFIC PLACE

www.pacificplace.com
Crammed with high-end designer outlets, this huge mall houses upscale brands including Dunhill, Ermenegildo Zegna, Versace, Shanghai Tang and Jimmy Choo. Also at Pacific Place, a number of local retailers sell casual separates.
🔲 E10 ✉ 1 Pacific Place, 88 Queensway ☎ 2844 8900 ⏰ Daily 10am–midnight 🚇 Admiralty

PICTURE THIS

www.picturethiscollection.com
This fascinating shop sells old-time posters, prints, books and maps. The colonial era is well served, as is the mainland Maoist era and the vintage travel posters and ephemera are a delight.
🔲 D10 ✉ Shop 212, 2/F, Prince's Building, 10 Chater Road, Central ⏰ Mon–Sat 10–7, Sun 12–5 🚇 Central

UPPER LASCAR ROW (CAT STREET)

A flea market set alongside more expensive shops and selling the same kind of bric-a-brac, records and curios, along with a few antiques.
🔲 B9 ✉ Off Queen's Road West, Sheung Wan ⏰ Daily 11–6 🚇 Sheung Wan

W. W. CHAN & SONS

www.wwchan.com
Mens suits made by this classy tailor have a life-span of about 20 years and will be altered free of charge at any point during that time. Once they have your measurements, you can order another suit from home.
🔲 C10 ✉ Unit B, 8th floor, Entertainment Building, 30 Queen's Road Central, Central ☎ 2366 9738 ⏰ Mon–Sat 10–7 🚇 Central

WINDSOR HOUSE COMPUTER PLAZA

www.windsorhouse.hk
A collection of specialist computer shops retailing hardware and software. Stores look more sophisticated than those in Sham Shui Po.
🔲 H10 ✉ 10th–12th floors, The In Square, Windsor House, 311 Gloucester Road, Causeway Bay ⏰ Daily 10–10 🚇 Causeway Bay

---

QTS

Look for the Quality Tourism Services (QTS) logo—a large, gold Q encircling a black Chinese character—in shop windows. This logo means that the shop has been accredited by the Hong Kong Tourism Board (HKTB) and is committed to certain standards. These include providing clear product and price information and also rectifying complaints should anything happen to go wrong.

Entertainment and Nightlife

BLCK BIRD
www.theblckbird.com
With its wood panelling and red leather, this classy bar reimagines the colonial-era gentlemen's club. The bar menus include some top whiskies and British ale.
⊞ C10 ⊠ 6th Floor, 8 Lyndhurst Terrace, Central ☎ 2545 8555 ⏱ Daily 3pm–1am ⊜ Central

CARNEGIE'S
www.carnegies.net
An interesting nightspot where the music shifts genre regularly but is often from local bands.
⊞ F10 ⊠ 53 Lockhart Road, Wan Chai ☎ 2866 6289 ⏱ Mon–Sat 11am–3am, Sun 5pm–2am ⊜ Wan Chai

DICKENS BAR
A Dickensian place that's one of Hong Kong's best bars. Bands change constantly—Irish, West Indian, Indonesian and Filipino—and there's jazz on Sunday afternoons.
⊞ G10 ⊠ Lower Ground Floor, Excelsior Hotel, 281 Gloucester Road, Causeway Bay ☎ 2837 6782 ⏱ Sun–Thu noon–1am, Fri–Sat noon–2am ⊜ Causeway Bay

DRAGON-I
www.dragon-i.com.hk
Still trendy after many years, the coolest club in Hong Kong is the place to be seen and is a magnet for the celebrity class. There's a bar, restaurant and a terrace overlooking busy Wyndham Street.

Happy hour is 6pm–9pm.
⊞ C10 ⊠ Upper ground floor, The Centrium, 60 Wyndham Street, Central ☎ 3110 1222 ⏱ Mon–Sat noon–late ⊜ Central

DROP
www.drophk.com
This is a seriously cool place to be and comes highly recommended by locals and visitors alike. It's very small and so has a members-only restriction on weekends, which is loosely enforced. Early evening it's a cocktail lounge, serving fresh fruit cocktails. DJs play later.
⊞ C10 ⊠ On Lok Mansion, 39–43 Hollywood Road, Central ☎ 2543 8856 ⏱ Tue 7pm–3am, Wed 7pm–4 am, Thu 7pm–4am, Fri–Sat 10pm–5am, Sun 8pm–2am ⊜ Central

---

CANTONESE OPERA

Dating back to the 12th century, this is a highly stylized but very energetic art form. The basic story lines follow the local myths. Characters wear startling make-up and gorgeous clothes. Though the Cantonese songs and accompaniment are loud and discordant to Western ears, the acrobatics and swordfights can be stunning. Watch it as a spectacle rather than a story. The audience chats, wanders about and sometimes joins in.

FOUR SEASONS SPA
With luxury private treatment rooms available, and a wide choice of therapies, you could easily pass away a day here enjoying facilities such as a vitality pool, flotation tank or aromatherapy massage.
⊞ C9 ⊠ 8 Finance Street, Central ☎ 3196 8888 ⏱ 8am–10pm ⊜ Central

FRINGE CLUB
www.hkfringe.com.hk
The Fringe Club is Hong Kong's main venue for non-mainstream performance art, as well as interesting drama workshops. During the Arts Festival alternative offerings are usually staged.
⊞ C10 ⊠ 2 Lower Albert Road, Central ☎ 2521 7251 ⏱ Mon–Thu noon–midnight, Fri, Sat noon–3am ⊜ Central

HONG KONG ACADEMY FOR PERFORMING ARTS
www.hkapa.edu
This arts school next to the Arts Centre has different-size theaters, plus an outdoor venue.
⊞ E10 ⊠ 1 Gloucester Road, Wan Chai ☎ 2584 8500 ⊜ Wan Chai

HONG KONG ARTS CENTRE
www.hkac.org.hk
Drama and music of diverse kinds take place here.
⊞ F10 ⊠ 2 Harbour Road,

Wan Chai ☎ 2582 0200
🚇 Wan Chai

HONG KONG CITY HALL

www.cityhall.gov.hk
The stage, auditorium and recital hall here host a wide variety of local and visiting artists. It's a popular place to watch Cantonese Opera (see panel opposite).
➕ D10 ✉ 5 Edinburgh Place, Central ☎ 2921 2840
🚇 Central

INSOMNIA

www.liverockmusic247.com
This place has been around long enough to have collected a loyal clientele. It has two bars and live music after 10.30pm. Happy hours 5–9. The place fills up in the early hours and especially so on weekends. All-day (and night) menu of simple dishes.
➕ C10 ✉ Ho Lee Commercial Building, 38–44 D'Aguilar Street, Central ☎ 2525 0957 🕐 Mon–Sat 9am–6am, Sun 2pm–5am
🚇 Central

MCSORLEY'S ALE HOUSE

www.mcsorleys.com.hk
Old-fashioned English pubs have played second fiddle to plush cocktail bars in recent years. This unpretentious ale house proves the battle is not yet lost. The selection of ales and bitters is second to none.
➕ C10 ✉ 355 Elgin Street,

SoHo, Central ☎ 2522 2646
🕐 Daily 11am–2am
🚇 Central then Mid-Levels Escalator

MO BAR

One of Hong Kong's chicest and best-loved hotel bars where you can get sumptuous cocktails. It's previously hosted low-key musical sets by visiting superstars.
➕ C10 ✉ Ground floor, Landmark Mandarin Oriental, 15 Queen's Road Central, Central ☎ 2103 0077 🕐 Daily 7am–1.30am
🚇 Central

RED

www.pure-red.com
Within the IFC mall, Red has a bar and restaurant, and an outdoor patio with sweeping views of both the harbor and the Central city skyline. There's live jazz on Thursday nights. Happy hour 6pm–9pm.
➕ D9 ✉ 4th Floor, IFC Mall, 8 Finance Street, Central ☎ 8129 8882 🕐 Mon–Wed

ISLAND NIGHTLIFE

Lan Kwai Fong, in Central, is where the see-and-be-seen crowd spends their money on overpriced drinks. Wan Chai, once seedy, is now one of the hippest nightlife areas in town. SoHo (South of Hollywood Road) is a popular dining and drinking area for expats. Stanley is more relaxed and meditative than other areas.

11.30am–midnight, Thu 11.30am–1am, Fri–Sat 11.30am–3am, Sun 11.30–10
🚇 Central

SENSE 99

www.sense99.com
This arts hangout is in a lovely heritage building. Indie tracks play upstairs while below guests are invited to play the drums and assortment of stringed instruments. Bohemians will love it.
➕ C10 ✉ 2nd–3rd Floor, 99 Wellington Street, Central ☎ 9466 4695 🕐 Fri–Sat only 9pm–4am 🚇 Central

SEVVA

www.sevva.hk
A chic and expensive restaurant, bar and lounge, with views over Statue Square (▷ 42), Sevva is surrounded by some of Hong Kong's most famous buildings. Low-slung comfy sofas allow the views to be enjoyed in style.
➕ D10 ✉ 25th Floor, Prince's Building, 10 Chater Road, Central ☎ 2537 1388 🕐 Daily noon–midnight
🚇 Central

STAUNTON'S WINE BAR & CAFÉ

www.stauntonsgroup.com
Packed to the gills most nights, this trendy and buzzing bar can be easily found by the SoHo Escalators.
➕ C10 ✉ 10–12 Staunton Street ☎ 2973 6611
🕐 Mon–Fri 10am–late, Sat–Sun 8am–late 🚇 Central

Restaurants

PRICES

Prices are approximate, based on a 3-course meal for one person.

$$$ over HK$700
$$ HK$300–HK$700
$ under HK$300

AL'S DINER ($$)

First-rate sirloin from the US goes into the fair-sized burgers. There's lots of 1950s chrome and neon, and a juke box churns out period songs.

➕ C10 ✉ Room F, Ground floor, Winner Building, 27–37 D'Aguilar Street, Central ☎ 2869 1869 🕔 Sun–Wed 11.30am–1am, Thu 11.30am–2am, Fri–Sat 11.30am–4am 🚇 Central

AMIGO RESTAURANT ($$$)

www.amigo.com
Spanish setting, French fare (*filet de sole Marquis, crevettes au gruyère*). Set meals are less expensive and less formal at lunchtime.

➕ G11 ✉ Amigo Mansion, 79A Wong Nai Chung Road, Happy Valley ☎ 2577 2202 🕔 Daily 12–3, 6–midnight 🚋 Tram from Central

BLUE BUTCHER ($$)

www.bluebutcher.com
Come here if you love meat—in particular dry aged beef—and cocktails. The emphasis is on inventiveness and punchy flavor both in the food and the drinks, carefully crafted by well-trained

mixologists. Subdued lighting and sharp design create an exciting club-like atmosphere.

➕ C9 ✉ 108 Holltwood Road, Central ☎ 2613 9286 🕔 Daily noon–late 🚇 Central

BRASSERIE LE FAUCHON ($$)

www.lefauchon.com.hk
The prices here are lower than other French restaurants around the territory but the quality remains high. The food is prepared by expertly trained local chefs using French ingredients and tastes fantastic. The interior is a relaxing, cool and light space. All round an enjoyable place to come.

➕ C10 ✉ Ground floor, 45 Elgin Street, Central ☎ 2526 8318 🕔 Daily 12–3, 6pm–midnight 🚇 Central

DIM SUM

The most traditional of Cantonese meals, dim sum is served from early morning to late afternoon in Cantonese restaurants all over the city. The dishes arrive in bamboo baskets piled high on a tray or trolley. As the servers circulate with the trolleys, just point at whatever takes your fancy. Popular dumplings include *har gau* (shrimps), *pai kwat* (spare ribs) and *woo kok* (vegetarian). You pay according to how many dishes you consume.

BRASSERIE ON THE EIGHTH ($$$)

Superb French fare—in small portions—with excellent service and lovely views.

➕ E11 ✉ 8th floor, Conrad International Hotel, Pacific Place, Admiralty ☎ 2521 3838, Ext. 8270 🕔 Mon–Sat 12–3, 6.30–11, Sun 11–3, 6.30–11 🚇 Admiralty

CAMMINO ($$)

Bringing a little taste of Italy to the heart of Causeway Bay, this restaurant works overtime at making you feel you are somewhere else. Great Italian food from the various regions of Italy in an intimate, quiet environment.

➕ G10 ✉ 1st Floor, The Excelsior Hotel, 281 Gloucester Road, Causeway Bay ☎ 2837 6780 🕔 Mon–Sat 12–2.30, 6–11, Sun 11–3, 6–11 🚇 Causeway Bay

CAPRICE ($$$)

Lavish and exquisite, this restaurant carries the prestige and allure of two well-earned Michelin stars. If your wallet can take the strain and you're lucky enough to secure a reservation then you will be rewarded with food and service of the highest quality, along with a magnificent art nouveau-styled setting and great harbor views.

➕ D9 ✉ Four Seasons Hotel, 8 Finance Street, Central ☎ 3196 8888 🕔 Daily 12–2.30, Mon–Sun 6–10.30 🚇 Central

COYOTE ($$)

www.coyotebarandgrill.com

Slurp down one of the 56 varieties of margarita, and to soak it up launch into a monstrous plate of *nachos simpaticos*.

🔲 F10 ✉ 114–120 Lockhart Road, Wan Chai ☎ 2861 2221 🕐 Daily 11.30am–midnight 🚇 Fortress Hill

DA PING HUO ($$)

Da Ping Huo is quite an unusual but charming private dining option. In addition to doing the waiting and cooking, the chefs may even serenade guests with Sichuanese opera before they depart. Mainly set menus.

🔲 C10 ✉ Lower ground, 49 Hollywood Road, Central ☎ 2559 1317 🕐 Daily 12.30–2.30pm, 6.30–11.30pm 🚇 Central

EL CID ($$)

www.kingparrot.com

El Cid is a very well-established Spanish restaurant, great for a long tapas evening but with a full Spanish menu, too. Wandering musicians serenade you as you eat. There is another restaurant in Causeway Bay.

🔲 H10 ✉ Ground floor, Florida Mansion, 9–11 Clevelnd street, Causeway Bay ☎ 2576 8650 🕐 Mon–Sat noon–1am, Sun noon–3, 6–midnight 🚇 Causeway Bay

GOLDFINCH RESTAURANT ($)

This time warp dining institution conjures the charm and ambience of 1960s Hong Kong. It's one of the few remaining restaurants which offer western meals such as steak and chips or cream of chicken soup, cooked in a style that is unmistakably Hong Kong. It's hardly gourmet fare but it's well worth visiting for the experience.

🔲 H10 ✉ 13–15 Lan Fong Road, Causeway Bay ☎ 2577 7981 🕐 Daily 11am–11.30pm 🚇 Causeway Bay

ICARAMBA! ($$)

www.caramba.com.hk

Spicy Mexican food with Chinese overtones is served up with plenty of tequila at this buzzing little spot in chic SoHo. Try the tasty tortilla chips. Reserve in advance for weekends.

🔲 C10 ✉ 26–30 Elgin Street, Central ☎ 2530 9963 🕐 Daily noon–midnight 🚇 Central

INDONESIAN RESTAURANT 1968 ($$)

www.ir1968.com

Serving up Indonesian favourites such as *nasi goreng* and *gado gado* since 1968, this old favourite has now moved from its historic home in Causeway Bay to Central but remains a destination for lovers of high quality, well-priced Southeast Asian cuisine.

🔲 C10 ✉ 5th Floor, The L Place, 139 Queen's Road Central, Central ☎ 2577

9981 🕐 Daily noon–midnight 🚇 Central

JIMMY'S KITCHEN ($$)

www.jimmys.com

Its history stretches back to the 1920s, venerable for Hong Kong, and its menu can be relied on for its signature goulash, borscht and stroganoff. Comfortable and traditional with equally reliable service.

🔲 C10 ✉ South China Building, 1 Wyndham Street, Central ☎ 2526 5293 🕐 Daily 12–3, 6–11 🚇 Central

JUMBO FLOATING RESTAURANT ($$$)

www.jumbo.com

Alone, this highly decor-ated boat is a tourist attraction in itself, but try the excellent res-taurant on board. It's a night out that begins with a free ferry ride in a small *sampan* across the harbor.

🔲 Farther afield map ✉ Jumbo Lungdom, Shan Wan Pier Drive, Aberdeen ☎ 2553 9111 🕐 Daily 11am–11.30pm 🚌 7, 70 from Central Bus Terminal

LOBSTER BAR AND GRILL ($$$)

Swanky, relaxed place with live bands playing to serenade you. Innovative modern European menu—try bluefin tuna with asparagus and egg-plant (aubergine) salad or the seared chicken breast with scallops and fennel. Nice bar, too.

🔶 E11 ✉ 6th Floor, Island Shangri-La, Pacific Place, Supreme Court Road, Central ☎ 2820 8560 ⏰ Daily 12–3, 6.30–10 🚇 Central

MAN WAH RESTAURANT ($$$)

Unlike most Chinese restaurants, the Man Wah is dimly lit, intimate and elegant, as you would expect in one of Hong Kong's best hotels. The food is excellent and worth the money.

🔶 D10 ✉ 25th Floor, Mandarin Oriental Hotel, 5 Connaught Road, Central ☎ 2825 4003 ⏰ Daily 7am–11am, Mon–Fri 12–3, 6.30–11 🚇 Central

MAXIM'S PALACE ($$)

www.maxims.com.hk
One of the few places where you can enjoy dim sum from hand-pushed trolleys, this is a vast dim sum institution, very popular for family brunch on Sundays. Prices are reasonable and there are great harbour views.

🔶 D10 ✉ 3rd Floor, City Hall, 5–7 Edinburgh Place, Central ☎ 2521 1303 ⏰ Mon–Sat 11–3, 5.30–11, Sun 9–3, 5.30–11 🚇 Central

THE PAWN ($$)

www.thepawn.com
This 19th-century pawn shop opened as a restaurant-bar in 2008 and underwent an overhaul in 2014 when

acclaimed British chef, Tom Aikens, joined the team. It's modern British cuisine in the main room, and there's also a lounge bar and rooftop garden to enjoy.

🔶 F11 ✉ 62 Johnston Road, Wan Chai ☎ 2866 3444 ⏰ Daily noon–midnight 🚇 Wan Chai

PEAK CAFÉ BAR ($)

www.cafedecogroup.com
This bar and café cannot be missed from the giant Mid-Levels Escalator route that crosses the center of SoHo. Inside is an interesting mixture of old-world Chinese decor, Gothic stonework and sparkling chandeliers.

🔶 C10 ✉ 9–13 Shelley Street, Central ☎ 2140 6877 ⏰ Mon–Fri 11am–2am, Sat 9am–2am, Sun 9am–midnight 🚇 Central

---

CHOPSTICKS

● Hold one chopstick between your thumb joint and the tip of your third finger.

● Hold the other chopstick between the tip of your thumb and the tips of your first and second fingers.

● Keep the first chopstick rigid. Move the second one up and down to grab food.

● Put food from the serving dish on top of rice, hold the bowl close to your mouth and push the food in with the chopsticks.

TANDOOR RESTAURANT ($$–$$$)

www.tandoorhk.com
A classy restaurant with rosewood furniture, lunch and dinner buffets and a wide-ranging menu. Try the betelnut-based desserts.

🔶 C10 ✉ 1st floor, Lyndhurst Tower, 1 Lyndhurst Terrace, Central ☎ 2845 2262 ⏰ Daily 12–2.30pm, 6–10.45 🚇 Central

TOKIO JOE ($$)

www.lkfe.com
Very trendy spot in Lan Kwai Fong serving good sushi and sashimi, as well as filled rolls and hot dishes. The same company has two more Japanese places in the area, Kyoto Joe and Joe's Yaki, which are more like teppanyaki bars.

🔶 C10 ✉ 16 Lan Kwai Fong, Central ☎ 2525 1889 ⏰ Mon–Sat 12–2.30, 6.30–11, Sun 6.30–11 🚇 Central

YUNG KEE RESTAURANT ($$)

www.yungkee.com
This long-standing favorite among local people is known as *the* place to eat Cantonese cuisine in the area. Yung Kee has a list of prestigious awards to support this belief. The restaurant is highly visible in the heart of the Central district, with a large glamorous shop front and valet parking.

🔶 C10 ✉ 32–40 Wellington Street, Central ☎ 2522 1624 ⏰ 11–11 🚇 Central

Less glamorous than its neighbor over the water, densely populated Kowloon is where the real daily life of Hong Kong happens. Shops are thick on the ground and if you have a hankering for real Chinese food this is where you'll find it.

Kowloon Walled City Park

TOP **25**

This park stands on the site of the former Walled City

KOWLOON TOP 25

THE BASICS

➕ H2
✉ Junction of Tung Tau Tsuen and Tung Tsing roads, Kowloon
🕐 Daily 6.30am–11pm
🚇 Lok Fu
♿ Good
🎟 Free

HIGHLIGHTS

● Pretty, quiet space in the middle of Kowloon
● Turtle and goldfish ponds
● Artistic topiary
● Renovated administrative building

TIPS

● This is a great place to bring a picnic.
● If you have your own chess pieces, you can have a game on the park's large Chinese chessboards.

Once the most notorious, lawless and poverty-stricken place in Hong Kong, Kowloon Walled City is now a manicured park, filled with pavilions, topiary and shady walks. Even the shrubs have been cut and shaped into animal figures.

From ruin to park In 1898, when Britain leased the New Territories from China, Kowloon Walled City was a Chinese garrison and was never included in any agreement. The two countries bickered over its jurisdiction for almost 100 years while the area became ever more ramshackle, with blocks of tenements raised without any kind of planning, nonexistent sanitation and frequent outbreaks of disease. During World War II the Japanese knocked the actual walls down to extend the old Kai Tak airport and thousands of illegal immigrants from China found a post-war refuge there. The two governments finally reached a settlement over the area in 1987, the 30,000 inhabitants were rehoused and the buildings were flattened, archaeologists rummaged around and finally a park was built in the ruins. The park is complete with pagodas, a Chinese zodiac garden, a mountain view pavilion and a hilltop pavilion.

Historic survivor One of the original buildings of the fort, the Yamen, dating back to the 19th century, has been restored and now holds a display of photos and other items concerning the history of the Walled City. Also discovered in the clearance were the stone plaques that marked the south gate of the Walled City.

Museum of Art

A beautifully laid-out series of galleries contains displays of exquisite Chinese calligraphy and painting, both traditional and modern, many stunning ancient artifacts and a collection of jade, ivory and pottery.

Chinese antiquities The museum has seven galleries; four contain Chinese antiquities, local artists' work and pictures that are of historical note as well as artistic worth. The thousands of exhibits in the Chinese antiquities section range from rhino-horn cups to burial goods and lavish tomb adornments; of particular interest are two large Tang dynasty (AD618–906) tomb guardians in the form of mythical beasts. The jade and ivory carvings in the decorative arts gallery are lovely.

Art galleries The best gallery is the one containing old pictures and prints of Hong Kong. It is hard to believe that the sandy beaches and jungle-filled hills could have become such a different kind of jungle in so short a space of time. It is a revelation of just how far the colony has come since the early 19th century.

Modern art The works in the contemporary art gallery are divided into decades, and it is particularly interesting to see the development of local art since the 1950s. There is also a collection of calligraphy and Chinese paintings, and a special gallery for international exhibitions. Between galleries, leather armchairs facing the enormous corridor windows allow you to enjoy the waterfront vista.

THE BASICS

www.lcsd/gov.hk/CE/Museum/Arts

➕ F8

✉ 10 Salisbury Road (next door to Hong Kong Cultural Centre)

☎ 2721 0116

🕐 Mon–Wed, Fri 10–6, Sat–Sun 10–7

🍴 Museum café

🚇 Tsim Sha Tsui

🚌 Tsim Sha Tsui bus station

⛴ Star Ferry from Wan Chai and Central to Tsim Sha Tsui

♿ Excellent

💰 Inexpensive; free Wed

❓ Museum bookshop

HIGHLIGHTS

● Han-dynasty pottery watchtower
● Tang-dynasty tomb guardians
● Translucent rhino-horn cups
● Painting of Wyndham Street
● Model of Guangzhou

Museum of History

TOP 25

This museum covers thousands of years of Hong Kong's history

THE BASICS

http://hk.history.museum

🔢 F7/G7

✉ 100 Chatham Road South, Tsim Sha Tsui

☎ 2724 9042

🕐 Mon, Wed–Sat 10–6, Sun 10–7

🍴 Café in museum

🚇 Tsim Sha Tsui East

🚌 5, 5C, 8 from Star Ferry

♿ Excellent

💲 Inexpensive (free Wed)

❓ Guided tours in English twice daily on Sat, Sun

HIGHLIGHTS

● The photographic collection

● Reconstructions of a tea shop, grocer's, barber's and cinema from the 1960s

● The re-created street from the early years of the last century with tram, boat, herbalists and more

● Reconstruction of the Bogue forts used in the Opium Wars

This gem of a museum, both user-friendly and informative, is a good place to spend an hour or two, especially as the curators frequently introduce new touring shows and exhibits.

Prehistory to the handover When the administrative body of HK SAR built this new $390 million history museum you had to wonder at how they might choose to rearrange the history of the island now the Brits had left. But have no fear—the museum is an excellent portrayal of the area from prehistory to the handover. The displays are interactive, with sounds and smells, and there are even walk-through exhibits like a Hakka family dwelling or an early tram.

Exhibits The natural history section documents most of the wildlife that has ever roamed these parts, while the archaeology area, covering about 6,000 years of history, tells the story of the island's earliest settlers. Most of the objects uncovered at Lei Cheng Uk (▷ 67) are here, too. There's an ethnography section explaining where all Hong Kongers originated from (but not much on more recent immigrants). The real interest of the museum though, is its account of more modern history. There are exhibits on the Japanese occupation (laid out as an air-raid shelter), Hong Kong's development and even a bit about what has happened since it became one of China's SARs. Stamps, old documents and a huge photographic collection make a visit to this fascinating museum anything but dull.

Science Museum

The Science Museum is one of Hong Kong's most popular attractions. In such a modern city, some of the 500 major exhibits feel a bit old-fashioned these days, but children will still love them.

Still popular Exhibitions include objects from the past as well as explaining how everyday items function, and some focus on the science and technology particularly relevant to Hong Kong. The museum's 18 galleries on four floors contain thousands of exhibits, most of them interactive, especially in the children's areas. Topics cover all aspects of science but it's the sheer scale of some of the exhibits that makes the science interesting. In one gallery a DC3 plane hangs from the ceiling, while a kinetic energy machine rises through all four floors of the museum and sends hundreds of balls pulsing around a metallic labyrinth.

For children The museum is definitely a child-oriented place and on weekdays hordes of them come here in school parties, although perhaps that's half the fun of it. Two exhibits are in particular demand here—a car linked up to a video screen where children can try to drive around the computer-simulated road in front of them and a similar setup with a whole light aircraft. Exhibits cover the entire spectrum of science-related subjects, from electricity and magnetism to a breakdown of what you eat. There are robot arms to operate, buttons to push and a scary machine that calculates the minute-by-minute increase in the world's population.

THE BASICS

http://hk.science.museum
⊞ F7/G7
✉ 2 Science Museum Road, Tsim Sha Tsui East
☎ 2732 3232
🕐 Mon–Wed, Fri 1–9, Sat– Sun 10–9
🍴 Café
🚇 Tsim Sha Tsui East
🚌 5, 5C, 8 from Star Ferry
♿ Good
✋ Moderate (free Wed)

HIGHLIGHTS

- Simulated interactive rides
- Giant energy tower
- Irresistible knobs to press
- Watching the school parties swarm onto the exhibits

TIPS

- School parties usually arrive mid-afternoon.
- Sunday is a very popular day for families.
- The Museum of History is close by if you want to make a day of it.

Space Museum

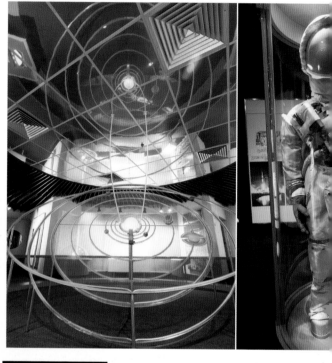

HIGHLIGHTS

- IMAX shows
- Mercury space capsule
- Hall of Space Science
- Solar telescope
- Planetarium show
- Hall of Astronomy

TIPS

- Some of the interactive exhibits have height and weight restrictions.
- If there is a typhoon or a black rainstorm warning, the museum will close.

This museum, which has one of the world's most advanced planetariums, is fascinating for kids, with plenty of hands-on exhibits, a *Mercury* space capsule and daily Space Theatre shows.

Layout and IMAX The museum's oval, pink building, built in 1980 by the Architectural Services Department, is in itself stunning. Inside are three exhibitions: the Hall of Astronomy, the Hall of Space Science and, the most popular, the Stanley Ho Space Theatre with its 75ft (23m) screen. If you haven't seen an IMAX film before, then seize the chance here. You sit back in tilted seats and gaze ahead and up at a screen that covers most of the ceiling and front wall. The shows here alternate between star shows using a star projector and IMAX shows from around the

A solar system display in the Hall of Astonomy (below left); a replica of a protective suit used by Apollo *astronauts on the moon landing (below middle) and a model of* Space Shuttle Columbia *in the Hall of Space Science (below right)*

world. The size of the screen allows an almost 360-degree panorama.

Exhibition halls The Hall of Space Science includes bits of moon rock, the actual *Mercury* space capsule piloted by Scott Carpenter in 1962, and lots of information about China's current space program. In the Hall of Astronomy there is a solar telescope where you can look directly at the sun. Did you know that it was ancient Chinese astronomers who were the first to spot Halley's Comet and the first to chart the movements of the stars? The interactive simulators include a gyroscope and models allowing you to launch spaceships, land a craft on the moon, take a moon walk or go hang gliding. This is a great place for visitors with children and those interested in space. Outside is a statue garden.

THE BASICS

www.hk.space.museum

🚩 F8

✉ 10 Salisbury Road (next to Hong Kong Cultural Centre), Tsim Sha Tsui

☎ 2721 0226

🕐 Sat–Sun 10–9, Mon, Wed–Fri 1–9

🚇 Tsim Sha Tsui

🚌 Tsim Sha Tsui bus station

⛴ Star Ferry from Central and Wan Chai to Tsim Sha Tsui

♿ Excellent

💲 Inexpensive; free Wed

❓ Children under 3 are not allowed in the IMAX

Star Ferry

HIGHLIGHTS

● Shops in Tsim Sha Tsui ferry terminal
● Vista to east and west along shipping lane
● Panoramic views of Hong Kong Island
● Hong Kong Maritime Museum
● Views of Peak and Mid Levels

The Star Ferry journey has to be one of the world's most spectacular sea crossings. You get a panoramic view of the harbor as you tack around dredgers, launches and all the other vessels.

Looking back The journey time on the Star Ferry, which has been operating between Kowloon and Hong Kong Island since 1898, is less than 10 minutes on a good day, but the views of the cityscape on both sides of the harbor are excellent—and all for HK$2.50 (less for the lower deck). The ferry terminal on the Tsim Sha Tsui side sits beside the incongruous Hong Kong Cultural Centre (1989), with its windowless, smooth-tiled surface (▷ 67). As the ferry sets off to Hong Kong Island, you can see the long pink-and-black striped outlines of the Museum of Art (▷ 55).

Riding the Star Ferry across Victoria Harbour is something every visitor to Hong Kong should experience

CENTRAL & WAN
中 區 及 灣 仔

Looking forward On the island itself, the stunning architecture of the reclaimed shoreline spikes the sky. The most eye-catching section begins with the Convention and Exhibition Centre, which juts out beside the Wanchai Pier and is framed by Central Plaza (▷ 26). Next door is the Central Government Complex and the Prince of Wales Building, home to the Chinese People's Liberation Army. To the right, I.M. Pei's Bank of China Tower is clearly visible beside the soaring monolith of the Cheung Tak Centre. Finally, behind Central's Star Ferry Pier is the IFC complex, with Two IFC, at 1,362ft (415m), the tallest building on Hong Kong Island. The excellent Hong Kong Maritime Museum (open daily) occupies three floors within Central Ferry Pier 8 and is well worth a visit. The dozen-plus galleries trace Hong Kong's long connection with the sea.

THE BASICS

www.starferry.com.hk

➕ E8

✉ Salisbury Road, Tsim Sha Tsui (Kowloon); Man Yui Street, Central (Hong Kong Island); Sea Front Road, Wan Chai (Hong Kong Island)

☎ Hotline: 2367 7065

🕐 Daily 6.30am–11.30pm. Office: 8.30am–6.30pm

🍴 Cafés, bakeries at Central ferry terminal gate

🚇 Tsim Sha Tsui (Kowloon); Central, Wan Chai (Hong Kong Island)

♿ Lower decks more accessible

💲 Inexpensive

Symphony of Lights

HIGHLIGHTS

● Harbor trip
● The cool of the Tsim Sha Tsui promenade
● Occasional pyrotechnic additions to the show
● The view beyond the harborfront to the Peak

TIPS

● Several tour companies offer 1.5-hour, drinks-included tours of the harbor.
● Star Ferries' tour (no drinks) is the least expensive at HK$170 for 1 hour.

Victoria Harbour has to be one of the most amazing sights of a trip to Hong Kong. Each evening a stunning sound-and-light show takes place creating a vibrant frenzy along the waterfront.

Dazzling display Impressive though it has always been, Victoria Harbour is even more striking since the introduction of a Symphony of Lights. It is a stirring experience to stand and watch this 18-minute performance by the buildings along the waterfront on Hong Kong Island and Kowloon. Every day at 8pm the exteriors of 46 of the city's major buildings glow with a myriad vivid colors, with the use of a wide range of architectural lights to draw the eye along the waterfront. Best viewed from Tsim Sha Tsui, the spectacle sees one build-ing after another light up, highlighting its outline or

changing its appearance altogether. With the addition of several buildings Kowloon-side, the lights and lasers reach across the harbor, turning the whole area into a dazzling display. A narration and music are broadcast each night along the Avenue of Stars, while onlookers from Tsim Sha Tsui and Golden Bauhinia Square in Wan Chai can tune into the narration by radio (English channel available on 103.4FM). On certain special occasions the light display is complemented by rooftop pyrotechnic displays on some buildings. You can also take one of the harbor cruises and listen to the narration and music piped aboard.

Take an evening stroll The striking display is recognized by the *Guinness Book of Records* as the largest permanent sound-and-light show in the world.

THE BASICS

www.tourism.gov.hk
/symphony

➕ F8

🕗 8pm–8.18pm

🚇 Tsim Sha Tsui, Wan Chai

♿ Good

🎟 Free

Temple Street

TOP 25

Grab a bargain at Temple Street Night Market

THE BASICS

🚇 E6

✉ Temple Street, Kansu Street, Reclamation Street, Kowloon

🕐 Jade market: 10–5. Temple Street market: 4pm–midnight. Vegetable market: early morning and early evening

🍴 Seafood restaurants and hawker area on Temple Street

🚇 Jordan

♿ Good

🎫 Free

HIGHLIGHTS

● Fresh fish for sale
● Fortune-tellers
● Chinese medicine shops
● Shops selling traditional Chinese wedding clothes
● Jade market
● Yau Ma Tei Typhoon Shelter, to the west
● Racks of T-shirts
● Exotic vegetables in vegetable market

At about 7pm each night, stands sprout on either side of this street and are hung with T-shirts, lingerie, jeans and other goodies. Earlier in the day, nearby stalls do a brisk trade in jade.

After dark The market is full of bargains—silk shirts, leather items, jeans and T-shirts. Nothing on sale is really indigenous as locals rather than visitors are the buyers. After about 2pm the street is closed to traffic as the stalls are set up. Restaurants line the street to the north and south of the main market throng and pull plastic tables and chairs onto the street after dark. This is one of few places where it's still possible to eat under the stars in downtown Hong Kong.

Jade for sale Close by, near the junction of Battery and Kansu streets under an overpass, is the jade market. Here, hundreds of stands sell all kinds of jade, which comes in many shades besides green—from white through to purple. Locals spend the afternoon bargaining over prices, which range from inexpensive to a king's ransom.

Still more In adjoining streets are vegetable and fruit sellers, shops selling fabrics and traditional red-embroidered Chinese wedding outfits and many Chinese medicine shops. If you are lucky, you may catch a Cantonese opera performance, around the Tin Hau Temple to the north of the street. As you walk through the market, look for people playing the age-old game of mahjong in the backs of shops or in corners.

Look across the harbor to (below) from the Waterfront Promenade (below right)

Waterfront Promenade

The views of Hong Kong Island and the harbor are outstanding all along the length of this promenade on the Kowloon waterfront.

Avenue of Stars Even before the creation of the Avenue of Stars the Waterfront Promenade was an excellent place for an evening's stroll, close to the chaos of Nathan Road but serene, and, above all, relatively unpopulated, especially toward its eastern end popular with old fishermen and canoodling lovers. Nowadays the 0.25-mile (400m) Avenue of Stars, a tribute to the 100 years or so of movie making in Hong Kong, draws the crowds. Represented here are some of the people responsible for the huge success of the industry. Lots of the stars have sunk their handprints into the cement blocks set into the ground, while there are a few others yet to turn up and oblige.

Statues There are also statues of the stars and a giant model of the statuette given out at the Hong Kong Awards ceremony each year. All the big names are here plus some you may never have heard of. Accompanying the plaques is a series of pillars that tell the history of film making. The lifelike statue of Bruce Lee was built from funds donated by his fans.

Weekends On weekends you will see wedding couples posing by the statues with the skyline of Hong Kong Island behind them. On Saturday evenings there are free music performances.

THE BASICS

⊞ F8
✉ Salisbury Road
🍴 Nearby
🚇 Tsim Sha Tsui
♿ Excellent
🎫 Free

HIGHLIGHTS

● Statue of Bruce Lee
● The view of the harbor
● Watching people posing by the statues
● The quieter eastern end

TIPS

● The evening is the best time to visit.
● Find a spot on the Avenue of Stars to watch the Symphony of Lights.

More to See

CLOCK TOWER
www.amo.gov.hk/en/monuments_43.php
The 148ft (45m) clock tower is all that remains of the Kowloon–Canton Railway Station—once the final stop of a rail network that stretched back to Europe.
➕ E8 ✉ Salisbury Road 🍴 Nearby 🚇 Tsim Sha Tsui ♿ Excellent

HONG KONG CULTURAL CENTRE
www.hkculturalcentre.gov.hk
Designed by the government's architectural services department in 1989, this is one of Hong Kong's most controversial buildings. It has a huge sloping roof that is matched by the dome of the nearby Space Museum, and is uniformly pink. The building is also windowless—rather odd as it would have one of the most stunning views in the world. Inside, it is very modern, especially the sparse auditoria with their apparently unsupported balconies. At the rear is a waterfront walkway.
➕ E/F8 ✉ Salisbury Road, Tsim Sha Tsui ☎ 3185 1612 🚇 Tsim Sha Tsui 🖐 Free

KOWLOON MOSQUE
www.kowloonmosque.com
Built on the site of an earlier 19th-century one, this is the largest mosque in Hong Kong.
➕ F7 ✉ Corner of Nathan and Haiphong roads ☎ 2724 0095 to arrange a visit ⊘ Closed to general public 🍴 Nearby 🚇 Tsim Sha Tsui

KOWLOON PARK
www.lcsd.gov.hk/parks/kp/indexc.html
Kowloon Park is full of fun things to do. There's an open-air and an indoor swimming pool, an aviary, a Chinese garden and much more. In the morning you can watch people practising t'ai chi.
➕ E7 ✉ Nathan Road ⊘ Daily 5am–midnight 🍴 Cafés and restaurants in Nathan Road 🚇 Tsim Sha Tsui ♿ Poor 🖐 Free

LEI CHENG UK TOMB MUSEUM
www.lcsd.gov.hk/ce/Museum/History/en/lcuht.php
Although built over an ancient Han dynasty tomb, this little museum is now surrounded by high-rise

Kowloon Mosque (above)

The Clock Tower (left)

Lei Cheng Uk Tomb Museum (right)

apartments, creating a continuity between the living and the dead, spanning 2,000 years.

➕ Off map at D1 ✉ 41 Tonkin Street, Sham Shui Po ☎ 2386 2863 🕐 Mon–Wed, Fri and Sat 10–6. Closed 25–26 Dec and first 3 days of Chinese New Year 🚇 Cheung Sha Wan 🚌 2 from Star Ferry to Po On Road ♿ Good access to museum displays but not to tomb 🎫 Free

MONG KOK

Mong Kok's crowded streets, tenements and markets are well worth experiencing. The Bird Garden, the Ladies Market, the Flower Market and the Goldfish Market are all very popular.

➕ F3 🚇 Mong Kok MTR, KCR ♿ Poor

NATHAN ROAD

Named after Sir Matthew Nathan, a governor of Hong Kong in the early 20th century, the road is 3.2 miles (5km) long. The southern stretch is known as the "Golden Mile", reflecting local real estate prices.

➕ F7 🍴 Many 🚇 Tsim Sha Tsui ♿ Poor

SKY100

www.sky100.com.hk

On the 100th floor of the ICC (International Commerce Centre) is the Sky100 observation deck which gives 360° views of the city. Only guests at the luxury Ritz Carlton Hong Kong hotel are allowed any higher. Rising to 1,588ft (484m), the ICC is Hong Kong's newest tallest building.

➕ D6 🚇 100th Floor, ICC, 1 Austin Road West, Kowloon ☎ 2613 3888 🕐 Daily 10–9 🚇 Kowloon 💰 Moderate ♿ Good

WEST KOWLOON PROMENADE

www.westkowloon.hk

This large sculpted parkland is a pleasant open space with a lovely wooden promenade. Use an Octopus card (▷ 119) to hire a SmartBike, from one of two hire points, to get around.

➕ D7 ✉ West Kowloon Cultural District ☎ SmartBike: 6182 3481 🕐 Park Daily 6am–11pm; SmartBike hire Mon–Fri 2–9, Sat–Sun 10–7 🚇 Kowloon 💰 Park free; SmartBike moderate ♿ Good

Bustling Nathan Road (left)

Sky100 (below)

Symphony of Lights and a Pub Crawl

An evening stroll along the waterfront of TST followed by some of the best places to eat and drink in Kowloon. Start the walk at 8pm.

DISTANCE: 1 mile (1.5km) **ALLOW:** 45 minutes, plus drinking time

START

TSIM SHA TSUI STAR FERRY TERMINAL
➕ E8 ⛴ Star Ferry

END

HILLWOOD ROAD
➕ F6 🚇 Jordan

❶ Head toward the Clock Tower (▷ 67), which is the best place to watch the Symphony of Lights (▷ 62) at 8pm. Follow the waterfront past the Hong Kong Cultural Centre (▷ 67) and the Museum of Art (▷ 55).

❷ Head down the Avenue of Stars promenade (▷ 65). Take in the amazing views across the waterfront.

❸ Double back toward the Space Museum (▷ 58–59) on Salisbury Road. Cross Salisbury Road via the underpass to arrive at the southern end of Nathan Road. Head north.

❹ At the Chingling Mansions, turn left down Peking Road to the One Peking Road building. Head up to the top floor for a cocktail at Aqua Spirit (▷ 73).

❽ The bars here have a more local feel and some strange titles.

❼ Head for the district of SoHo: turn right onto Observatory Road, left onto Kimberly, stay on the left onto Austin Avenue and keep an eye peeled for the stairs on the left that lead up to Hillwood Road.

❻ Wander north through the park, then bear right to rejoin Nathan Road around the Kimberley Road junction. Take the next left up Knutsford Steps into Knutsford Terrace. Here you should enjoy a well-earned rest in one of the lively bars. This street also has a number of great restaurants that you should consider.

❺ Returning down Peking Road, turn left at Hankow Road to reach Maphong Road and the southern entrance to Kowloon Park.

KOWLOON WALK

Shopping

BROADWAY

www.broadway.com.hk
This is one of the biggest branch of a Hong Kong-wide electronics and electrical chain that sells everything from washing machines to electric razors. Most major brands are available at marked down prices, which are more or less fixed, although you might get a free gift thrown in. You can get a good idea here of a sensible local price, and then move on to serious haggling in some smaller, pushier place if that's what you really want to do.

🔢 E4 ✉ Ground–3rd floor, 79 Argyle Street, Mong Kok ☎ 2381 9819 🕐 Daily 9.30–11 🚇 Mong Kok

CHINESE ARTS AND CRAFTS (HK) LTD.

www.cachk.com
You can find some beautiful things here—pottery, silks, embroideries, carved gemstones, clothes, furniture, carpets, tea, jewelry, statues and novelties.

🔢 E8 ✉ Star House, 3 Salisbury Road, Tsim Sha Tsui ☎ 2735 4061 🕐 Daily 10–9.30. Closed Chinese New Year 🚇 Tsim Sha Tsui

ELISSA COHEN JEWELLERY

www.elissacohen.com
This place is a bit more exciting than the standard jewelry shop chains. Lots of individually designed pieces but higher prices to match.

🔢 F7 ✉ 209 Hankow Centre, 5–15 Hankow Road ☎ 2312 0811 🕐 Mon–Fri 9–5.30, Sat 9–1 🚇 Tsim Sha Tsui

FESTIVAL WALK

www.festivalwalk.com.hk
One of Hong Kong's most attractive malls, Festival Walk is a weekend destination in itself for many locals, with its own cinema, ice-rink and the largest bookshop in town, in addition to the expected boutiques. It's right beside the Kowloon Tong metro interchange.

🔢 F1 ✉ 80–88 Tat Chee Avenue, Kowloon Tong ☎ 2844 2222 🕐 11–10 🚇 Kowloon Tong

FORTRESS

www.fortress.com.hk
A major rival of Broadway, offering cameras, sound equipment, camcorders, electronics, electronic games and so on, all at fixed prices. There are dozens of branches throughout the city, but this one is good for reconnaissance before setting off on a major

CHINESE EMPORIA

Chinese emporia are perhaps the most diverse shops in the world. They range from markets, government-owned department stores selling Made-in-China basics, to private stores stocking merchandise from around the world.

haggling trip. Buy here and enjoy a hassle-free holiday, but if you like the cut and thrust of bargaining, then this should at least be your first stop to check prices.

🔢 E7 ✉ Shop 333A, 333B, 335–7, 3rd floor, Ocean Centre, Harbour City, Canton Road, Tsim Sha Tsui ☎ 3101 1413 🕐 Daily 10.30–9.30 🚇 Tsim Sha Tsui

GRANVILLE ROAD

Small boutiques selling mid-priced youth labels line this trendy street in Tsim Sha Tsui. There are many more within the Rise Shopping Arcade and nearby Beverly Shopping Centre on Chatham Road South. Inspiration, and custom, is provided by the nearby Hong Kong Polytechnic University which boasts one of Asia's top design schools.

🔢 F7/G7 ✉ Granville Road 🕐 Daily 10–9 🚇 Tsim Sha Tsui

HARBOUR CITY

www.harbourcity.com.hk
Compromising five inter-linking malls, this goliath building has branches of upmarket international and local boutiques such as Givenchy and Swank, as well as an excellent Marks and Spencer and local chain stores such as G2000.

🔢 E8 ✉ 3-27 Canton Road, Tsim Sha Tsui, Kowloon ☎ 2118 8666 🕐 Daily 10–10 🚇 Tsim Sha Tsui

JUST GOLD
www.justgold.cc
Popular Hong Kong chain of reasonably priced jewelry stores. Fixed prices and a bit on the kitsch side but stress-free.
🚹 F7 ✉ Prestige Tower, 23–25 Nathan Road, Tsim Sha Tsui ☎ 2117 0490 🕐 Daily 10.30–10 🚇 Tsim Sha Tsui

LADIES' MARKET
The long stretch of Tung Choi Street, between Argyle Street and Dundas Street, is home to the daily Ladies' Market, so called for the enormous amount of female fashions. There are also home furnishings, CDs, accessories and trinkets available. It's cramped and claustrophobic, and haggling is essential, but great fun.
🚹 E3 ✉ Tung Choi Street 🕐 Daily 2–10.30 🚇 Mongkok

MONG KOK COMPUTER CENTRE
www.mongkokcc.com
This small shopping block is crammed with tiny shops that spill out into the teeming corridors. The vendors are knowledgeable and catalogs of prices are on display. Hardware is mostly Asian-made: computers, monitors, printers and add-on boards. Warranties are usually only for Asia, but prices are competitive.
🚹 E4 ✉ 8–8a Nelson Street, Mong Kok 🕐 Daily 10–10 🚇 Mong Kok

ORIENTAL ARTS JEWELRY
You'll find a wide selection of jade at this sophisticated shop within the Peninsula Hotel's upscale arcade. Also, for those who like to make their own jewellery, there is a large range of beads and stones available to purchase loose.
🚹 F8 ✉ Mezzanine, Peninsula Hotel Shopping Arcade, Salisbury Road, Tsim Sha Tsui ☎ 2369 0820 🕐 Daily 10–8 🚇 Tsim Sha Tsui

RISE COMMERCIAL BUILDING
This place is filled with small boutiques carrying the handiwork of local designers, as well as affordable imports from Japan and Korea.

MADE TO MEASURE
Perhaps the most distinctive aspect of men's clothes in Hong Kong is the number and quality of tailors and the excellent prices of their products compared to almost everywhere. If you intend to have a suit made in Hong Kong, you should make finding a tailor that you like a priority, since the more time and fittings he can have the better the suit will be: a good tailor can make a suit in as little as 24 hours, but a few days will yield a better, less expensive suit. Some tailors offer a mail-order service.

🚹 F7 ✉ 5–11 Granville Circuit, Tsim Sha Tsui 🕐 Various 🚇 Tsim Sha Tsui

SAM'S
www.samstailor.com
This tailor is another Hong Kong institution, numbering the Duke of Kent among its clientele.
🚹 F7 ✉ Burlington Arcade K&L, 90–94C Nathan Road, Tsim Sha Tsui ☎ 2367 9423 🕐 Mon–Sat 9.40–7 🚇 Tsim Sha Tsui

TSE SUI LUEN JEWELLERY
www.tslj.com
There are branches of this store around the city, selling fairly traditional designs of jewelry, watches and more. Branches in Queen's Road, Central, Causeway Bay and Nathan Road.
🚹 F7 ✉ Shop A&B, Ground floor, 190 Nathan Road, Tsim Sha Tsui ☎ 2926 3210 🕐 Daily 10–10.30 🚇 Jordan

YUE HWA CHINESE PRODUCTS EMPORIUM
www.yuehwa.com
A more basic and everyday shop than the other, more centrally located Chinese emporia. Look for inexpensive but beautiful dinner services, embroideries, pricey and inexpensive jewelry, workaday silk items and Chinese herbal medicines.
🚹 F6 ✉ 301 Nathan Road, Kowloon ☎ 3511 2222 🕐 Daily 10–10 🚇 Jordan

Entertainment and Nightlife

ALL NIGHT LONG
www.websitetocome
Newly opened live music bar in the little haven of good places to drink off Knutsford terrace.
➕ F6 ✉ 9 Knutsford Terrace ☎ 2367 9487 🕐 Sun–Thu 4pm–5am, Fri-Sat 4pm–6am 🚇 Tsim Sha Tsui

AQUA SPIRIT
www.aqua.com.hk
A quite breathtaking cocktail lounge above two of Kowloon's trendiest restaurants. The views toward Hong Kong Island are some of the best you'll see. An essential stop for out-of-towners.
➕ F7 ✉ 30F, 1 Peking Road, Tsim Sha Tsui, Kowloon ☎ 852 3427 2288 🕐 Daily 5pm–2am 🚇 Tsim Sha Tsui

BAHAMA MAMA'S
www.mhihk.com
All pub crawls on this side of the water end around here somewhere and this is as good a place as any. Nice mix of locals and *gweilos*. Entrance charge on club nights but worth the investment.
➕ F7 ✉ 4–5 Knutsford Terrace ☎ 2368 2121 🕐 Mon–Thu 5pm–3am, Fri, Sat 5pm–4am, Sun 6pm–2am 🚇 Tsim Sha Tsui

CHUAN SPA
www.chuanspa.com
Complete with private treatment rooms, a range of luxurious products and professional staff, Chuan Spa is a great place to relax. Enjoy a massage or facial in the peaceful surroundings while enjoying the serenity of the spa's waterfalls.
➕ E4 ✉ Level 41, Langham Place Hotel, Mong Kok ☎ 3552 3510 🕐 Daily 10am–11pm 🚇 Mong Kok

DELANEY'S
www.delaneys.com.hk
The design re-creates a Victorian Irish store and pub, and there's live traditional music and Irish food—even Guinness. There's a sister branch in Luard Road, Wanchai, which has a Sunday evening jam session.
➕ F7 ✉ Basement, Mary Building, 71 Peking Road, Tsim Sha Tsui ☎ 2301 3980 🕐 Daily 8am–2.30am 🚇 Tsim Sha Tsui

HONG KONG CULTURAL CENTRE
www.hkculturalcentre.gov.hk
The premier venue for orchestral music, ballet and theater. There's usually an international event of one genre or another on the schedule.
➕ E8 ✉ 10 Salisbury Road, Tsim Sha Tsui ☎ 3185 1612 🚇 Tsim Sha Tsui

HONG KONG PHILHARMONIC ORCHESTRA
www.hkphil.org
A large, international orchestra with regular performances, often on weekends, in the Cultural Centre (▷ 67) and City Hall. Ticket prices increase when a prestigious conductor arrives.

NED KELLY'S LAST STAND
The best place in Hong Kong for traditional and Dixieland jazz, belted out by a resident band. Expect a convivial atmosphere, pub food and no cover charge.
➕ E7 ✉ 11a Ashley Road, Tsim Sha Tsui ☎ 2376 0562 🕐 Daily 11.30am–2am 🚇 Tsim Sha Tsui

OZONE
OZONE claims to be the highest bar in the world and few who have perched on the outdoor terrace, 118 floors above the city, would argue. The cocktails are super-expensive but it's worth it for the view. No sandals.
➕ D6 ✉ 118th Floor, Ritz-Carlton Hong Kong, ICC, 1 Austin Road West, Kowloon ☎ 2263 2270 🕐 Mon–Wed 5pm–1am, Thu 5pm–2am, Fri 5pm–3am, Sat 3pm–3am, Sun noon–midnight 🚇 Kowloon

KOWLOON ENTERTAINMENT AND NIGHTLIFE

Restaurants

AQUA ROMA & AQUA TOKYO ($$$)

www.aqua.com.hk
Located on the top floor of Tsim Sha Tsui's tallest port-front tower (1 Peking Road), Aqua Roma combines Italian cuisine with panoramic views over Victoria Harbour. On the other side, Aqua Tokyo has a teppanyaki bar and booths overlooking Kowloon's gritty cityscape. The Aqua Spirit cocktail bar—the source of the Buddha Bar-style beats—is just above on the mezzanine floor. No shorts or sandals.
🔢 F7 ✉ 29/F, 1 Peking Road, Tsim Sha Tsui, Kowloon ☎ 3427 2288 🕐 Mon–Sat 12–2.30, 6–11, Sun 12–3, 6–11

AVA ($$$)

Located on the 38th floor of the Hotel Panorama, this restaurant boasts magnificent Victoria Harbour views and an intimate environment. Come here for a cocktail at dusk, or enjoy the global cuisine after dark when the city sparkles. Request a window seat at all costs.
🔢 F7 ✉ 38F, Hotel Panorama, 8A Hart Avenue,
Tsim Sha Tsui ☎ 3550 0262 🕐 Daily 6.30am–10.30pm

THE BOSTONIAN ($$)

Fresh fish, brought to your table for you to choose, plus imaginative preparations and bright decor suggest California—never mind the eatery's name. If you come for the lunch buffet, plan for a light dinner.
🔢 E7 ✉ Langham Hotel, 8 Peking Road, Tsim Sha Tsui ☎ 2132 7898 🕐 Daily 12–3, 6.30–11 🚇 Tsim Sha Tsui

BULLDOG'S BAR AND GRILL ($)

www.bulldogsbarandgrill.com.hk
Union Jacks abound in this pub and restaurant with live music nights, giant plasma screens to watch the football and a menu that includes a breakfast fry-up, fish-and-chips and more exotic dishes.

🔢 G7 ✉ Shop G5, Tsim Sha Tsui Centre, 65 Mody Road ☎ 2311 6993 🕐 Mon–Thu 11am–2am, Fri–Sun 11–4 Happy Hour 5–8pm 🚇 Tsim Sha Tsui

DAN RYAN'S CHICAGO GRILL ($$)

www.danryans.com
Traditional choices on the menu include clam chowder, potato skins, salads and baby back ribs in barbecue sauce. The burgers are universally recognized as excellent. Leave room for brownies or carrot cake. Be sure to make a reservation—this place is popular.
🔢 F1 ✉ Lower Ground, Festival Walk, Kowloon Tong ☎ 2735 6111 🕐 Mon–Thu 11–11, Fi 11–midnight, Sat10am–midnight, Sun 10–11 🚇 Kowloon Tong

DELHI CLUB ($)

Plush by Chungking Mansions standards and frequented by regulars—two good reasons for a feast here.
🔢 F7 ✉ Block C, Flat 3, 3rd floor, Chungking Mansions, 36–44 Nathan Road, Tsim Sha Tsui ☎ 2368 1682 🕐 Daily 12–3.30, 6–11.30 🚇 Tsim Sha Tsui

DIN TAI FUNG ($–$$)

www.dintaifung.com.hk
The Tsim Sha Tsui outlet of this ever-popular Taiwanese nationwide chain has remarkably earned itself a Michelin star. It's the best place in town to try *xiaolongbao*,

Shanghai's much-loved dumpling snack. Expect to queue on weekends.

🔢 E8 ✉ Shop 310, 3rd floor, Silvercord Centre, 30 Canton Road, Tsim Sha Tsui ☎ 2730 6928 🕐 Daily noon–midnight 🚇 Tsim Sha Tsui

FELIX ($$–$$$)

You'll find excellent contemporary cuisine in this chic, modern restaurant designed by Philippe Starck. Excellent Californian/Pan-Asian cuisine, featuring seasonal ingredients. The night city view from the wrap-around floor to ceiing windows is magical.

🔢 F8 ✉ 28th floor, Peninsula Hotel, Salisbury Road, Kowloon ☎ 2696 6778 🕐 Daily 6pm–10.30pm 🚇 Tsim Sha Tsui

FU WAH ($)

Basic decor, but very popular with the locals. No-one really speaks English, but don't worry– they do have an English menu. A wide variety of traditional Cantonese dishes and possibly the best pork and rice dishes in town. Also very good value for money so definitely worth a visit.

🔢 H5 ✉ 2Ground floor, Hurlingham Centre, 37–39 Ma Tau Wai Road, Hung Hom ☎ 2715 6864 🕐 Daily 7am–midnight 🚇 Hung Hom

GADDI'S ($$$)

One of Hong Kong's best restaurants is somewhere you'll remember, especially if you go at night when the chandeliers are sparkling and the band is playing. It's popular with Asian tourists for both its fine service and French food. Reservations are a must.

🔢 F8 ✉ 1st Floor, Peninsula Hotel, Salisbury Road, Tsim Sha Tsui ☎ 2696 6763 🕐 Daily 12–3, 6.30–11 🚇 Tsim Sha Tsui

GAYLORD INDIAN RESTAURANT ($)

www.mayfare.com.hk
The starters here are superb, and the breads and kebabs come fresh out of the tandoori oven. One of the best ways to try the food here is to have a lunch buffet. Cozy and pubby.

🔢 E7 ✉ 1st floor, Ashley Centre, 23–25 Ashley Road, Tsim Sha Tsui ☎ 2376 1001 🕐 Daily 12–2.30, 6–11 🚇 Tsim Sha Tsui

HARLAN'S ($$$)

www.jcgroup.hk/restaurants/harlans
A fine dining restaurant atop Hong Kong's tallest shopping mall. The indoor dining space is pleasant, but the standout draw is the wonderful balcony with views the length of Nathan Road to the harbour. Fare is mainly Mediterranean.

🔢 F7 ✉ Level 19, The ONE, 100 Nathan Road, Tsim Sha Tsui ☎ 2972 2222 🕐 Daily 12–2.30, 6–12.30 🚇 Tsim Sha Tsui

INAGIKU GRANDE ($$)

www.rghk.com.hk/dining
World-renowned tempura, sushi, teppanyaki and sashimi is served in this chic and quietly elegant restaurant located on the first floor of the luxury Royal Garden Hotel. Free parking for diners.

🔢 E7 ✉ 69 Mody Road, Tsim Sha Tsui East, Kowloon ☎ 2733 2933 🕐 Daily 12–3, 6–11 🚇 Tsim Sha Tsui

INANIWA UDON-NABE ($$)

www.taste-well.com
Sato Yosuke Udon was a specialty only the Meiji-period Japanese elite were able to enjoy. You can too in this fine restaurant, located at the foot of Hong Kong's (latest) tallest building.

🔢 D6 ✉ 2nd floor, Elements, 1 Austin Road West, West Kowloon ☎ 2196 8989 🕐 Mon–Sun 11–3.30, 5.30–10.30 🚇 West Kowloon

JIMMY'S KITCHEN ($$)

www.jimmys.com
Sister restaurant to the Hong Kong Island branch, this place has been around for decades (possibly with the same furniture). Redolent of the 1920s it serves home-cooked food with a European theme, including English oysters and Russian bortsch. A Hong Kong institution.

🔢 E7 ✉ South China Building, ground floor,

Kowloon Centre, 29 Ashley Road ☎ 2376 0327 ⊙ Daily 11.30–2.30, 6–11 🚇 Tsim Sha Tsui

KHYBER PASS ($)

If you are keen to venture into Chungking Mansions (▷ 75, panel), this 7th-floor mess hall is a good place to start your adventure. Seating is at long tables, prices are low and the north Indian food is pretty standard. Clean, basic and safe.

🔴 F7 ✉ 7th floor, Block E, Chungking Mansions, Nathan Road ☎ 2721 2786 (2782 2768) ⊙ Daily noon–3.30, 6–11.30 🚇 Tsim Sha Tsui

MEZZO GRILL ($$)

American-style steaks and seafood. The restaurant specializes in chargrilled dishes. Try the sole fillets wrapped in applewood smoked bacon.

🔴 F7 ✉ Regal Kowloon Hotel, 71 Mody Road, Tsim Sha Tsui ☎ 2313 8778 ⊙ Daily 12–3, 6–11 🚇 Tsim Sha Tsui

THE MISTRAL ($$$)

Enjoy a relaxed meal away from the Tsim Sha Tsui crowds, plus excellent pasta, pizza and other Italian dishes. Rustic Mediterranean furnishings.

🔴 G7 ✉ Basement floor 2, Grand Stanford InterContinental, 70 Mody Road, Tsim Sha Tsui East ☎ 2721 5161 ⊙ Daily noon–2.30, 6–10.30 🚇 Tsim Sha Tsui

NADAMAN ($$$)

The design is simple yet sophisticated, with a definite Japanese feel. There is a sushi bar available or you could reserve one of the booth tables for a more intimate meal. The extensive menu offers quality sushi, sashimi and tempura as well as other authentic Japanese cuisine. A chef's set menu is also available.

🔴 F7 ✉ Basement floor 2, Kowloon Shangri-La, 64 Mody Road, Tsim Sha Tsui ☎ 2733 8751 ⊙ Daily noon–2.30, 6–10.30 🚇 East Tsim Sha Tsui KCR, Tsim Sha Tsui MTR

SAGANO RESTAURANT ($$$)

The Japanese chefs at this restaurant in a Japanese hotel prepare distinctive kansai cuisine from around the Kyoto area. Don't miss the teppanyaki counter,

VEGETARIAN CHOICE

Vegetarian diners in Hong Kong are rarely disappointed, especially as there are many vegetarian options offered in the South Indian and, the more common, North Indian restaurants found throughout the city. A few vegetable dishes accompanied by *raita* (yogurt) and *naan* (puffed-up whole wheat), complemented by a lentil *dal* adds to a small feast for two.

where the chefs create intricate delicacies whilst juggling with their sharp cooking tools.

🔴 G7 ✉ 1st floor, New world Millennium Hong Kong Hotel, 72 Mody Road, Tsim Sha Tsui ☎ 2313 4215 ⊙ Daily 12–2.30, 6–10.30 🚇 Tsim Sha Tsui

WOODLANDS INTERNATIONAL RESTAURANT ($)

In the city's only Indian vegetarian restaurant, the decor is slightly spartan but the food is excellent. The *dosa* (rice-flour pancakes) and *thali* (set meals) are excellent and good value. Note: no alcohol is served here.

🔴 F7 ✉ Upper ground floor, Wing On Plaza, 62 Mody Road, Tsim Sha Tsui ☎ 2369 3718 ⊙ Daily 12–3.30, 6.30–10.30 🚇 Tsim Sha Tsui

YAN TOH HEEN ($$$)

Excellent, classy, Cantonese cuisine right on the waterfront. Gorgeous place settings in green jade. Lots of awards for its cooking and ambience. Excellent business lunch, hundreds of dim sum nibbles and 24 different types of fish on the menu.

🔴 F8 ✉ InterContinental Hotel, 18 Salisbury Road, Tsim Sha Tsui ☎ 2313 2323 ⊙ Mon–Sat 12–2.30, 6–11, Sun 11.30–3, 6–11 🚇 Tsim Sha Tsui

The vast bulk of the Special Administrative Region is here in this rural hinterland north of Kowloon, studded with new towns and traditional villages, and home to some spectacular parks, walking trails, wetlands, ancient temples and museums.

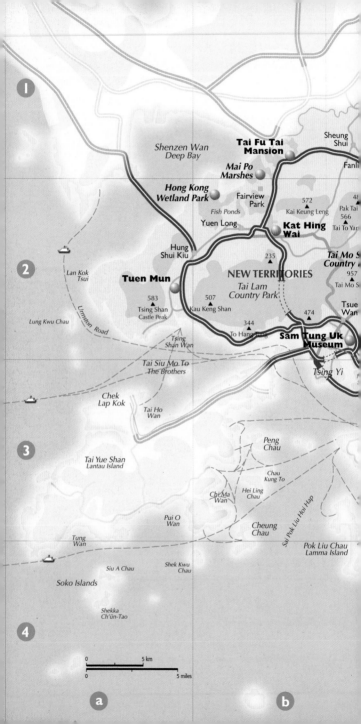

1

Shenzen Wan
Deep Bay

**Tai Fu Tai
Mansion**

Sheung
Shui

Fanli

*Mai Po
Marshes*

**Hong Kong
Wetland Park**

Fairview
Park

572
Kai Keung Leng

4
Pak Tai

Fish Ponds

Yuen Long

566
Tai To Yar

**Kat Hing
Wai**

Hung
Shui Kiu

235

**Tai Mo S
Country**

2

Lan Kok
Tsui

Tuen Mun

NEW TERRITORIES

957
Tai Mo S

583
Tsing Shan
Castle Peak

507
Kau Keng Shan

*Tai Lam
Country Park*

Lung Kwu Chau

Urmston Road

*Tsing
Shan Wan*

474

Tsue
Wan

*Tai Siu Mo To
The Brothers*

344
To Hang

**Sam Tung Uk
Museum**

*Chek
Lap Kok*

Tai Ho
Wan

Tsing Yi

3

*Peng
Chau*

Tai Yue Shan
Lantau Island

*Chau
Kung To*

*Chi Ma
Wan*

*Hei Ling
Chau*

*Pui O
Wan*

*Cheung
Chau*

Sai Pok Liu Hoi Hap

*Tung
Wan*

Pok Liu Chau
Lamma Island

Siu A Chau

Shek Kwu
Chau

Soko Islands

*Shekka
Ch'ün-Tao*

4

0   5 km

0   5 miles

a

b

492 ▲ Hung Fa Leng

Sha Tau Kok Hoi

Kat O Chau

Kat O Hoi

Tai Pang Wan
Mirs Bay

Luk Keng

486 ▲ Kwai Tau Leng

639 ▲ Wong Leng

Wong Wan Chau

Chek Chau

430 ▲

Plover Cove Reservoir

Tap Mun Chau

Tai Po

Chek Mun Hoi Hap

Tai Po Hoi
Tolo Harbour

Wu Kai Sha

481 ▲ Shek Uk Shan

468 ▲ Nam She Tsim

382 ▲ Sai Kung Peninsula

Ten Thousand Buddhas Temple

702 ▲ Ma On Shan

Sai Kung

Sai Kung Hoi

Pak Tam Chung

Tai Long Wan

Sha Tin

Ma On Shan Country Park

314 ▲

High Island Reservoir

Tai Wo Ping

577 ▲

Kau Sai Chau

ong Tai Temple

Chi Lin Nunnery

Ho Chung

Kwun Tong

▲602

Tai Po Tsai

HONG KONG

Tseung Kwan O

Ngau Mei Hoi

Tiu Chung Chau

Fu Tau Pun Chau

Sha Tong Hau Shan

Fo Shek Chau

Hang Hua

Yau Tong

344 ▲

Tsing Shui Wan

a Harbour

LOHAS Park

g Kong Island

Steep Island

Kwo Chau Kwan To

Tung Lung Chau

Pok Liu Hoi Hap

Sheung Sze Mun

Sung Kong

Lo Chau

Po Toi

c

d

Hong Kong Wetland Park

- Pui Pui, the celebrity crocodile
- The views across the wetlands from the viewing gallery
- The wobbly mangrove boardwalk

- The website's planner page makes your trip more productive.
- There is an indoor children's play area.

Opened to the public in May 2006, this huge artificial wetland area was created from some disused fishing ponds. The park now offers visitors an accessible and entertaining view of the varied and extremely colorful wildlife of the Mai Po Marshes.

Wetland ecology When they undertake new developments in Hong Kong they do it on a very big scale and the Wetland Park is no exception. Lying between the Mai Po Marshes (▷ 85) and the scarily big Tin Shui Wai New Town, this wetland, all 151 acres (61ha) of it, stands as a barrier protecting the marshes from encroachment by the town and a means by which locals and visitors alike can learn about the diverse ecology of the wetlands.

Tour the park on the wooden boardwalks and look out for the different kinds of plant, animal and marine life

The Wetland Interactive World The visitor center's exhibits provide information about the world's various wetlands and the impact humans have on them. The theater offers a global perspective, while the viewing gallery allows visitors to see the wetlands through telescopes and cameras located around the park.

On the boardwalks Outside, four wooden board-walks lead visitors around the various habitats of the park: through areas planted to attract specific insects, birds, butterflies, dragonflies and mangrove dwellers, to areas for creatures that live and hunt in the streams. A boardwalk crosses mangroves and there are three hides where you can watch the wildlife without being seen. The reserve is home to the celebrity crocodile Pui Pui, captured in 2003 and brought here in August 2006.

THE BASICS

www.wetlandpark.gov.hk

➕ b2

✉ Wetland Park Road, Tin Shui Wai

☎ 3152 2666

🕐 Mon, Wed–Sun 10–5

🍴 Café on ground floor

🚇 Tin Shui Wai (MTR) then light rail 705 Tin Shui Wai Circular to Wetland Park Station

♿ The center is accessible but boardwalks could be difficult

💰 Moderate

🛍 Shop

Ten Thousand Buddhas Temple

HIGHLIGHTS

● Thousands of small statues of Buddha
● Embalmed and gilded body of monastery's founder
● Statues of Buddha's followers
● Views over Sha Tin

TIPS

● Do not use flash photography inside the temple.
● Look out for wild macaques on the way up.

A half-hour train ride out of Hong Kong brings you to this striking temple set on a hillside overlooking the apartments, housing projects and towers of the satellite town of Sha Tin.

Bountiful Buddhas To reach the temple, take the train to Sha Tin and follow the signs. You must then climb 431 steps up the hillside. Every five steps or so is a life-size fiberglass Buddha to encourage you on your climb. Known locally as Man Fat Sze Temple, this Buddhist shrine has, since it was built between 1949 and 1957, become known as the Ten Thousand Buddhas Temple because of the matrix of small statues that decorate it. The statues, the donations of grateful worshippers over the years, are all different—some black, some covered in gold leaf—and each Buddha strikes a

different pose. There are, in fact, 13,000 or more Buddhas—but who's counting?

Panoramas and pagodas From the edge of the courtyard there are magnificent views over Sha Tin. The courtyard houses a tiered pagoda and the statues of some of Buddha's bright red followers, as well as five temples and four pavilions. Followers Manjusri and Samantabhadra occupy two of the pavilions. On the route up to the temple is another set of four temples, one containing Hong Kong's second-tallest Buddha statue, another the embalmed, gilded remains of Yuet Kai, who founded the Man Fat Sze Monastery and, despite his great age, personally carried some of the stones up to the site from the bottom of the hill. If there is a funeral taking place here, you will see paper gifts that are burned for the deceased in the afterlife.

THE BASICS

www.10kbuddhas.org (in Chinese)
➕ c2
✉ Close to Pai Tau Street, Sha Tin, New Territories
☎ 2691 1067
🕐 Daily 8–6. Particularly busy around Chinese New Year
🚇 Sha Tin
♿ None
🎫 Free, but donations welcome

Wong Tai Sin Temple

TOP 25

Wong Tai Sin Temple (below left) and a streetside stand at the temple (below)

THE BASICS

www.siksikyuen.org.hk

➕ c3

✉ Wong Tai Sin Estate; follow signs from MTR station

☎ Information: 2327 8141

🕐 Daily 7–5.30. Main temple is not always accessible

Ⓜ Wong Tai Sin (exit B2)

♿ Good

💷 Free (donations welcomed)

HIGHLIGHTS

● Main altar including painting of Wong Tai Sin
● Garden of Nine Dragon Wall
● Fortune-telling arcade
● Clinic block
● Stands outside selling windmills and hell money
● Chinese gardens at rear of complex
● Side altar in main temple dedicated to monkey god
● Incinerators for burning offerings

If temples were shops, then Wong Tai Sin Temple would be a supermarket. During Chinese New Year, you risk having your hair set on fire by hundreds of devotees waving joss sticks as they whirl from one deity to the next.

Wong Tai Sin This large Taoist temple, built in 1973 in Chinese style and situated among high-rise residential blocks, is dedicated to Wong Tai Sin, an ex-shepherd who was taught how to cure all ills by a passing deity. In modern-day Hong Kong, Wong Tai Sin is a very popular god, as he is in charge of the fortunes of gamblers. He can also be sought out by those who are ill or who have concerns about their health, and by people asking for help in business matters.

Symbolic interior The temple complex is vast, almost stadium-size, composed not just of the main temple, where Wong Tai Sin is represented by a painting rather than a statue, but also by turtle ponds, libraries, medicine halls and what is almost a small shopping mall of fortune-tellers. The temple is built to represent the geomantic elements of gold, wood, water, fire and earth. In the Yue Heung Shrine are fire and earth; gold is represented in the Bronze Luen Pavilion where the portrait of Wong Tai Sin is kept; and the Library Hall and water fountain represent wood and water respectively. The temple also caters to those who venerate Confucius, represented in the Confucius Hall, while Buddhists come here to worship the Buddhist goddess of mercy, Kuan Yin.

More to See

CHI LIN NUNNERY

www.chilin.org

Where the nearby Wong Tai Sin Temple (opposite) is always hectic, Chi Lin Nunnery offers Buddhist a place of calm, largely thanks to the beautifully landscaped Nan Lian Garden. The complex was rebuilt in the style of a palatial Tang dynasty complex only in 1990, but the all-timber nunnery buildings, built without the use of a single metal hinge or nail, make it a highly photogenic stop.

🔲 c3 ✉ 5 Chi Lin Drive, Diamond Hill, Kowloon ☎ 2354 1888 🕐 Daily 9–4.30; Garden 6.30am–7pm 🚇 Diamond Hill MTR (exit C2) 🖐 Free ♿ Poor

KAT HING WAI

The biggest of Hong Kong's clans, the Tangs, settled here hundreds of years ago, building walled villages as protection against bandits and pirates. Four hundred Hakka still inhabit the village of Kat Hing Wai.

🔲 b2 ✉ Kam Tin 🚇 Kam Sheung Road MTR ♿ Poor

MAI PO MARSHES

On the edge of mainland China and framed by the hazy, fume-filled sky-line of Shenzhen, the internationally protected Mai Po Marshes are home to thousands of rare and endangered birds—get some binoculars to view.

🔲 b1 ✉ Mai Po ☎ 2526 1011 🕐 Daily 9–6 🚇 Sheung Shui then a taxi 🚌 76K from Sheung Shui MTR station ♿ None 🖐 Moderate ❓ Reserve a visit in advance since numbers are limited. Refundable deposit required. Binoculars can be rented at the visitor center

SAI KUNG PENINSULA

This is the green lung of Hong Kong, containing the 18,772-acre (7,600ha) part of the Ma On Shan Country Park, a reservoir, the Maclehose walking trail, a marine park and the fourth highest peak in the territory. Start off at Sai Kung village, and go island hopping, windsurfing or walk the trails.

🔲 d2 🚇 MTR to Sha Tin then bus 299 to Sai Kung village or MTR to Diamond hill then bus 92

The Sai Kung Peninsula (above)

Women of Kat Hing Wai in traditional Hakka dress (right)

SAM TUNG UK MUSEUM

www.heritagemuseum.gov.hk

The simple lines of this ancient Hakka village stand out against the forest of high-rise housing blocks. The main hall is highly ornate; its original decorations have been restored to their original bright reds and greens. The other two halls, used for daily living, are more rustic. These now display farming equipment, period furniture and kitchen utensils.

🔢 b2 ✉ 2 Kwu Uk Lane, Tsuen Wan, New Territories ☎ 2411 2001 🕐 Mon, Wed–Sun 10–6 🚇 Tsuen Wan (exit E) ♿ Few 💰 Free ❓ HKTB Heritage tour, plus private tours

SHA TIN

Sha Tin is easily visited by train from Kowloon. In addition to a huge shopping and entertainment complex, there are restaurants, temples, Hong Kong's newest horse-racing track, mountain trails and a Tang walled village. Look out for the fountain opposite the station with its pretty display of water and lights.

🔢 c2 🍴 Many, especially in New Town Plaza 🚇 Sha Tin MTR ♿ Good

TAI FU TAI MANSION

Built around 1865, this traditional mansion has been fully restored; ceramic figurines decorate the facade, while the rooms contain plaster moldings and woodcarvings.

🔢 b1 ✉ Wing Ping, Tsuen, San Tin, Yuen Long 🕐 Daily 9–1, 2–5 🚇 Sheung Shui MTR then bus 76K

TAI MO SHAN COUNTRY PARK

www.afcd.gov.hk

This country park is home to Hong Kong's highest mountain and the beautiful Ng Tung Chai waterfalls.

🔢 b2 ✉ Tsuen Wan 🍴 Take a picnic 🚇 Tsuen Wan 💰 Free

TUEN MUN

Several interesting and historic Buddhist and Taoist monasteries can be found in Tuen Mun, such as Castle Peak, Ching Chung Koon and Miu Fat.

🔢 a2 🚇 Tuen Mun MTR West

Red altar in the Sam Tung Uk Museum (left)

Children playing outside Tai Fu Tai Mansion (below)

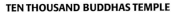

To Ten Thousand Buddhas Temple

This walk from Che Kung to the Ten Thousand Buddhas Temple goes via a shopping megatropolis in Sha Tin.

DISTANCE: 2.2 miles (3.5km) **ALLOW:** 2 hours (plus shopping time)

START

END

CHE KUNG TEMPLE MTR
🚉 c2 🚇 Che Kung Temple KCR

TEN THOUSAND BUDDHAS TEMPLE
(▷ 82–83) 🚉 c2 🚇 Sha Tin KCR

1 Leave the station (on the Ma On Shan line) by Exit B and go through the pedestrian subway crossing Che Kung Miu Road. Turn right and walk for 10 minutes.

2 At the Che Kung Temple be sure to turn the windmills for good luck. Che Kung, who protects against floods, stands dark red and shiny in the center of the temple.

3 Retrace your steps along Che Kung Miu Road to the pedestrian tunnel and follow signs to Tsan Tai Uk. This will lead you through a number of pedestrian tunnels.

4 You will know you have emerged at the right place when you see tennis courts on your left. The village of Tsang Tai Uk is now almost derelict.

8 At the MTR barriers turn right to exit New Town Plaza. Outside at the bus terminal take a left and head right and downward and turn left through Pau Tai village up toward the Ten Thousand Buddhas Temple.

7 Farther along, Lek Yuen bridge is on the right. Turn left here and climb the steps of the registry office to a podium. Cross to the walkway leading past Snoopy's World to New Town Plaza. Make your way to the MTR.

6 Use the subway to cross Lion Rock Road to Sha Tin Park opposite. The park is a pleasant place for a rest. Follow the river and exit the park through the north gate, passing the amphitheater on the right.

5 Return to the pedestrian tunnels. This time follow signs to the Hong Kong Heritage Museum to take you over the Lion Bridge across the Shing Mun river channel.

NEW TERRITORIES WALK

Shopping

SHA TIN

This area out toward the racecourse is full of small electronics shops, as well as branches of the major electrical outlets. Prices are likely to be marked and fixed. If you are looking for electronic goods you might also try the two department stores, Seiyu and Yaohan, in New Town Plaza. There are lots of reasonably priced clothes shops. Don't go on Sunday or you will find yourself among what seems like the entire population of the New Territories.

➕ c2 🍴 Restaurants in New Town Plaza 🚇 Sha Tin MTR

SHOPPING TIPS

Before leaving home, check prices on the kinds of items you may like to buy when you're in Hong Kong. Despite the city's reputation as a source of low prices on cameras and many types of electronic equipment, prices can sometimes be higher here than in the US. Shop around and try haggling a little, and avoid shops that do not display prices. If you do make a purchase, keep all receipts and original packaging. Unlike at home, however, many dealers won't accept returns.

TAI PO MARKET

Tai Po is a busy blend of malls, street markets and museums. The hub remains Fu Shin Street, where stalls sell everything from inexpensive clothes, cooking utensils and herbal remedies. The traditional wet market has been moved from here to nearby Heung Sze Wui Street. Meanwhile, the MTR station which takes the name is surrounded by the Uptown Plaza, if you want a more serene shopping experience.

➕ c2 ✉ Fu Shin Street 🕐 Fu Shin Street Market 10–10; Wet market 6am–9pm; 🚇 Tai Wo MTR

Entertainment and Nightlife

CLEARWATER BAY GOLF AND COUNTRY CLUB

www.cwbgolf.org

A par-70, 18-hole, pro-championship course. Visitors allowed weekday mornings only; a handicap certificate is required.

➕ c3 ✉ 139 Tai Mun Road, Clearwater Bay ☎ 2719 1595 🕐 Daily 7am–9pm 🚇 Hang Hau 🏌 Green fees HK\$1,800

KAU SAI CHAU PUBLIC GOLF COURSE

www.kscgolf.org.hk

At this public course there are three 18-hole courses—two were designed by Gary Player—and a driving range.

➕ d2 ✉ Kau Sai Chu, Sai Kung, New Territories ☎ 2791 3380 🕐 Daily 7am–8pm 🚇 Choi Hung, then bus 92 or Green Minibus No. 1A to Sai Kung Bus Terminal. Go to waterfront for the golf course's ferry for Kai Sai Cha 🏌 Green fees HK\$620–HK\$960

SHA TIN TOWN HALL

www.lcsd.gov.hk/stth

The large gray Town Hall at this New Territories community hosts many international artists, especially classical

orchestras. To visit, exit the Sha Tin station, walk through the shopping complex and, on the other side, is the Town Hall, next to the library.

➕ c2 ✉ 1 Yeun Wo Road, New Town Plaza, Sha Tin ☎ 2694 2509 🕐 Daily 7am–8pm (10pm on weekends) 🚇 Sha Tin MTR

SILVERSTRAND

One of three excellent swimming beaches with changing rooms, food stalls and BBQ stations.

➕ c3 ✉ Clearwater Bay Road, Sai Kung 🚇 Choi Hung then bus 92 or taxi

Restaurants

FOOD RESTAURANT

PRICES

Prices are approximate, based on a 3-course meal for one person.

$$$ over HK$700
$$ HK$300–HK$700
$ under HK$300

ANTHONY'S RANCH ($$)

www.anthonys-ranch.com
Specializing in Texas smoke-house cuisine, this expat-friendly Sai Kung restaurant majors in ribs, burgers, steaks and chops. The food is served up amid Wild West kitsch. There are bands on weekends and televised sport.

➕ Off Map c2 ✉ Ground floor, 28 Yi Chun Street, Sai Kung ☎ 2791 6113
🕐 Mon–Wed 11.30am–midnight, Thu–Fri 11.30am–2am, Sat–Sun 8.30am–midnight
🚇 Choi Hung MTR (exit C2) then 1A minibus

COSMOPOLITAN CURRY HOUSE ($)

A highly popular place in Tai Po, right beside the MTR, serving food from across Asia. Loud, noisy, and brash, it's a typical Hong Kong eatery.

➕ c2 ✉ 80 Kwong Fuk Road, Tai Po Market ☎ 2650 7056 🕐 Daily 11–11 🚇 Tai Po Market MTR

NAM SAN GOK ($)

This Korean restaurant in New Town Plaza (▷ 89) comes well recommended by locals.

Flaming traditional dishes such as Kimchee sit alongside a variety of moderate American-influenced dishes.

➕ c2 ✉ Shop 507, Level 5, New Town Plaza Phase 1, Sha Tin ☎ 2608 2172
🕐 Mon–Fri 11.30–3.30, 5.30–11, Sat–Sun 11.30–4, 5.30–11 🚇 Sha Tin MTR

SAKURADA ($$)

Classy Japanese place in the Royal Park Hotel. Food is prepared by Japanese chefs and teppanyaki is a specialty.

➕ c2 ✉ 8 Pak Hok Ting Street, Sha Tin ☎ 2694 3810 🕐 Daily 11.30–3, 6–11 🚇 Sha Tin MTR

LA TERRAZZA BAR AND GRILL ($$)

www.luprarestaurant.com./hongkong/terrazza.cfm
Located amid the rooftop greenery of Sha Tin Town Hall, La Terrazza is one of the few upscale Western restaurants in this part of Hong Kong. It's not overly posh, however, and the

EUROPE IN ASIA

Virtually every European cuisine is represented in Hong Kong and the food in the restaurants loses nothing from being transplanted to Asia. Locals tend to like the more expensive hotel restaurants, while younger Hong Kong couples prefer the more informal European-style places.

lunch sets are decent value for money.

➕ c2 ✉ Roof Garden, Sha Tin Town Hall, 1 Yuen Wo Road, Sha Tin ☎ 2940 2827
🕐 Mon–Fri 12–10, Sat–Sun 11–10 🚇 Sha Tin MTR

TUNG KEE SEAFOOD RESTAURANT ($–$$)

www.tungkee.com.hk
This popular Sai Kung restaurant is directly on the promenade and has plenty of outdoor tables for seaside dining on balmy evenings. This restaurant does great set meals for groups of more than two. You will find a second outlet on Hoi Pong Square.

➕ c2 ✉ 96–102, Man Nin Street, Sai Kung ☎ 2792 7453 🕐 Daily 9am–11pm

WONG'S KITCHEN AND CAFÉ ($)

If Sha Tin New Town Plaza gets you down, wander outside to this tiny café in Pau Tai village. Surrounded by paper products shops, this air-conditioned, functional, inexpensive pan-Asian place serves homemade Japanese and Western food as well as local dishes. From Sha Tin KCR follow the signs for Ten Thousand Buddhas Temple (▷ 82–83). You'll find Wong's Kitchen is just at the beginning of the ascent.

➕ c2 ✉ 28 Pau Tai village, Sha Tin ☎ 2601 3218
🕐 Daily 7am–10pm 🚇 Sha Tin MTR

Beyond Hong Kong Island itself are 260 or more outlying islands, many of them little more than uninhabited rocks, but several make for an exciting day out. One, of course, is home to the Tian Tan Buddha.

Farther Afield/Outlying Islands

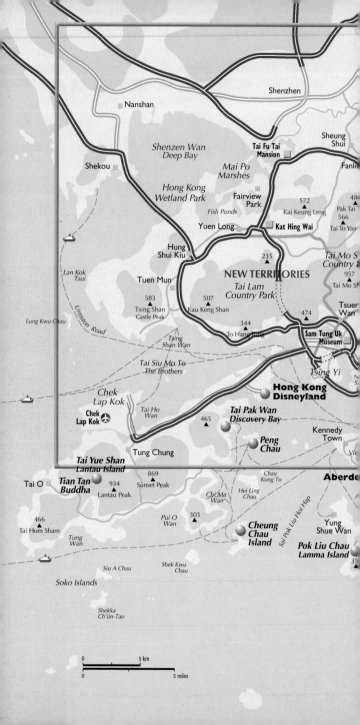

492
Hung Fa Leng

Sha Tau Kok Hoi

Kat O Chau

Kat O Hoi

Tai Pang Wan
Mirs Bay

Luk Keng

Wong Wan Chau

486
Kwai Tau Leng

Chek Chau

639
Wong Leng

Plover Cove
Reservoir

**Tap Mun
Chau**

430

Chek Mun Hoi Hap

Tai Po

Tai Po Hoi
Tolo Harbour

Wu
Kai Sha

481
Shek Uk Shan

468
Nam She Tsim

382

Sai Kung Peninsula

Tai Long
Wan

702
Ma On Shan

Ten Thousand
Buddhas Temple

Pak Tam
Chung

Sha
Tin

Sai Kung

Ma On Shan
Country
Park

Sai
Kung Hoi

High Island
Reservoir

314

Tai
Wo Ping

Kau Sai
Chau

577

Wong Tai
Sin Temple

Chi Lin Nunnery

Ho Chung

Kowloon
City

▲602

Kwun
Tong

Tai Po Tsai

Tiu
Chung Chau

Fu Tau
Pun Chau

KOWLOON

Tseung
Kwan O

Ngau
Mei Hoi

HONG KONG

Sha Tong
Hau Shan

Fo Shek
Chau

n Harbour

Hang Hua

Yau Tong

344

Tsing Shui Wan

LOHAS
Park

532

Steep
Island

Chai Wan

312

Kwo Chau
Kwan To

ng Kong Island

232

Tung Lung
Chau

Wong
Chuk Hang

Ocean
Park

Repulse
Bay

325

Stanley

Sheung Sze Mun

Sung
Kong

Pok Liu Hoi Hap

Lo Chau

**Po Toi
Island**

Cheung Chau Island

HIGHLIGHTS

● The bun festival
● Car-free walks around the island
● Sampan rides across the harbor
● Sandy beaches
● Inexpensive seafood

TIP

● The ferries from Central alternate between fast and slow—about 15 minutes' difference. There is no deck access on fast ferries.

Cheung Chau has two good beaches, lots of seafood restaurants, some interesting temples, caves, windsurfing equipment and bicycles for rent, good walks, no traffic and an annual bun festival.

Ferry to Cheung Chau An air-conditioned, first-class cabin with a bar and a sunny, open-air deck make the 40-minute ferry ride past speeding catamarans, scruffy sampans, vast tankers and tiny golden islands a relaxing treat. You could spend a couple of days on this car-free island, enjoying its beaches, eating seafood and wandering the footpaths. Cheung Chau is great for scenic walks along concrete paths (watch out for the little electric vehicles that cart goods around the island). To the north, a route leads you uphill to a reservoir from where there are excellent

views over the island. To the south, another road brings you to Sai Wan village where there is a Tin Hau temple and a footpath to the cave (so the story goes) of a pirate called Cheung Po-Tsai. From Sai Wan you can catch a sampan back to Cheung Chau village, a fun trip in itself.

The village In Cheung Chau village there are a few things to see and quite a lot to eat. Cheung Chau's main draw is the modern Pak Tai Temple (originally built in the 18th century), dedicated to the god who saved the island from plague. Each year the bun festival, which takes place over a week in summer, brings in thousands of visitors. There is a vibrant market selling seafood, vegetables and freshwater pearls to the 20,000 or so residents. Side streets are packed with fascinating shops.

THE BASICS

✚ See map ▷ 92–93
🚢 Outlying Islands Pier 5, Central: approximately half-hourly 24 hours (though only three ferries run between midnight and 6.10am)
♿ Difficult
👟 Moderate
❓ Tung Wan and Kwun Yam beaches have cafés

Hong Kong Disneyland

© Disney

HIGHLIGHTS

● Meeting favorite Disney characters and obtaining their autographs
● Light and fireworks show ("Disney in the Stars") daily each evening
● Live stage shows and 3-D cinema technology

TIPS

● Check the website for admission reductions at certain times.
● Tickets can be bought at the Hong Kong MTR station.

Meet your favorite Disney characters in Fantasyland, sail into darkest Africa and Asia on Adventureland's Jungle River Cruise and take a flight on a soaring space adventure in Tomorrowland.

Disney in Asia The second Disney Park to open in Asia, Hong Kong Disneyland is on Lantau Island and offers a great day out for young and old alike. Even if your view of Disneyland is a cynical one, when you actually get there you'll find it very hard not to smile at the many familiar figures and the magical atmosphere.

The magic There are seven main areas to explore (Fantasyland, Adventureland and Tomorrowland, Main Street USA, Grizzly Gulch, Mystic Point and Toy Story Land), each offering thrilling experiences,

© Disney

© Disney

© Disney

from climbing Tarzan's Treehouse, embarking on a 3-D adventure with Mickey or hurtling into the universe on Space Mountain. The latter has to be the best of the rides—a speeding roller coaster through deepest dark space, that plays some fascinating tricks on your senses.

Relaxation For more relaxing pursuits, you could enjoy some regional cuisine in one of the ten themed restaurants, or browse the range of souvenirs, bric-a-brac and nostalgic photographs for sale within the Main Street shops.

Shows and parades Throughout the day, you can watch one of the live musical stage shows with various Disney "celebrities," and every afternoon the vibrant "Disney on Parade" tours the park with musicians, dancers and brightly colored floats.

THE BASICS

www.hongkongdisneyland.com

🔂 See map ▷ 92–93

✉ Lantau Island

🕐 9–9 (may vary occasionally throughout the year)

🚇 Tung Chung line from Hong Kong station, then Disneyland resort line at Sunny Bay

💰 Expensive. Savings can be had at off-peak times

Tian Tan Buddha and Lantau Island

HIGHLIGHTS

- Tian Tan Buddha
- Tranquil monastery
- Views of the South China Sea and other islands
- Ngong Ping Skyrail
- Museum of Buddah's life (podium, 2nd level)

TIP

- Hong Kong Dolphin Watch (www.hkdolphinwatch.com) organizes trips to see the endangered pink dolphins of Lantau island every Monday, Friday and Sunday.

The 112ft-tall (34m), 250-ton bronze statue of Buddha on Lantau Island can be seen in his meditative pose from your aircraft as you descend into Chek Lap Kok airport.

Worth the trek Even after the airport was built, Lantau remained one of the largest green areas in Hong Kong. It is home to rare species such as the Hong Kong newt and the ayu, a stream-dwelling fish. The island's rocky coastline and jungle mountain scenery make it a bit of an outback. But this isolated outpost is home to almost 300 Buddhist monasteries, most of them tiny temples tucked away in remote areas. Po Lin (Precious Lotus) Monastery, halfway up the mountainside on the Ngong Ping Plateau was established by three monks in 1905 and is regularly restored, most

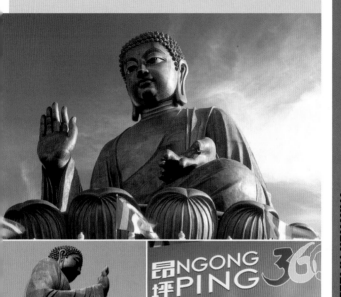

The gigantic bronze Tian Tan Buddha is a truly amazing sight

NGONG PING 36
您的身心啓迪之旅由此開始
Your Journey of Enlightenment begins

recently in 2013. The monastery's real attraction is the famous Tian Tan Buddha, completed in 1993, on the hilltop above the monastery. To get up close, you need to climb 268 steps. At the summit, you get a splendid view of Lantau.

Footpaths and beaches Despite the new developments on the island there are still miles of quite challenging unspoiled footpaths, as well as some pretty beaches on the eastern shores, the most accessible at Mui Wo, where the ferries from Central dock. On the south coast are Pui O and Cheung Sha, both accessible from Mui Wo by bus.

Skyrail An essential part of the Lantau experience is the Ngong Ping Skyrail cable car ride.—the 3.5-mile (5.7km) ride is spectacular. Beside the upper terminus is a faux-Tang dynasty village.

THE BASICS

www.plm.org.hk
🕇 See map ▷ 92–93
✉ Lantau Island
🕐 Monastery: daily 8–6.
Ngong Ping Skyrail Mon–Fri 10–6, Sat–Sun 9–6.30
🚇 Tung Chung and then bus 23 heading for Po Lin or Skyrail cable-car
🚢 Ferry to Mui Wo from Outlying Ferry Pier 6 (journey time approx 45 min), then bus 2
♿ Free. Skyrail moderate
❓ HKTB guided walks: Lantau Island–Tung Chung Valley

More to See

DISCOVERY BAY

"Disco" Bay, as those in the know like to call it, is a community of apartment-block dwellers, most of whom commute daily to Hong Kong Island. They enjoy car-free living and a long stretch of sandy white beaches. There are restaurants, shops and all the facilities a trendy settlement such as this requires, including the Discovery Bay Golf Club (open by prior arrangement for nonmembers on weekdays), plus all the trails of Lantau to wander at will. A catamaran takes about 25 minutes from Central or buses connect with Tung Chung MTR.

➕ See map ▷ 92–93 📷 Air-conditioned round-the-clock ferries take 25 min from Central

LAMMA ISLAND

A short ferry ride from the city, Lamma Island is car-free and offers a relaxing day out in relatively unspoiled countryside (if you ignore the massive, ugly power station and quarrying). Most people who visit do one of the pretty, moderately simple walks and end their day with dinner in one of the island's popular seafood restaurants. Ferries arrive at the island's biggest village, Yung Shue Wan, at the northwestern end of the island. There are restaurants, a bank, post office and Tin Hau temple here.

From Yung Shue Wan an hour-long, easy walk across the island brings you to Sok Kwu Wan (also accessible by ferry from Central), where the bulk of the seafood restaurants are located.

Another half-hour walk from Yung Shue Wan brings you to Mo Tat Wan, a tiny village, and the nearby beaches of Shek Pai Wan and Sham Wan. From Sok Kwu Wan a path leads you to the highest point on the island, Mount Stenhouse, a stiff climb rewarded with excellent views.

➕ See map ▷ 92–93 📷 Outlying Islands Pier 4, Central to Yung Shue Wan: half-hourly 6.30am–12.30am. Last returning ferry at 11.30pm. From Central to Sok Kwu Wan: 7.30am–11.30pm. Last returning ferry is 10.40pm 🖐 Free ♿ Poor

Gazing out to sea from Lamma Island

PENG CHAU

This small island to the east of Lantau is popular with day-trippers. Climb to the island's highest point, Finger Hill, at 311ft (95m), visit an 18th-century Tin Hau temple, explore the shops in the narrow lanes or sample the seafood in one of the restaurants. Five minutes from the village is Tung Wan, the island's only beach.

➕ See map ▷ 92–93 🍴 Inexpensive seafood restaurants in village 🚢 Outlying Islands Ferry Pier 6, Central: 7am–12.30am. Last ferry back at 11.30pm

PO TOI ISLAND

Although close to Hong Kong Island, this tiny rocky place is one of the least accessible of the islands. Ferries run only on weekends and there is nowhere to stay on Po Toi. It is possible to visit during the week if you hire a junk. The island has a Tin Hau temple and lots of quite challenging walks. It takes about two hours to walk right round the island. Po Toi is popular with picnickers on Sunday who come for the walks and for the Bronze Age

rock carving. There are a few seafood restaurants and a little beach at Tai Wan where the ferry docks. There was once a thriving village here, the only signs of which are the seafood places and some ruined houses. An excellent website (www.hkoutdoors.com) details a fine walk across the island.

➕ See map ▷ 92–93 🚢 Kaito Ferries operate from St. Stephen's Beach, near Stanley, on Sat, Sun. Ferries also run between Aberdeen and Po Toi on Tue, Thu, Sat, Sun and public holidays

TAP MUN CHAU

A tiny island off the Sai Kung Peninsula, Tap Mun Chau has a few scattered inhabitants who make their living from fishing. There are many pleasant walks and some sandy beaches with clean water for swimming. A Tin Hau temple, some semi-wild cows and bird life make up all there is to see. On weekdays you'll have the island to yourself.

➕ See map ▷ 92–93 🚢 2 ferries a day (3 Sat and Sun) from Ma Liu Shui Pier, near University MTR station. Last ferry: 5.30pm

Tin Hau Temple, Peng Chau Island (above)

Peng Chau (right)

Lantau Island

A walk across Lantau Island from Po Lin across natural woodlands, stark hillsides and a verdant valley to the new town of Tung Chung.

DISTANCE: 4.3 miles (7km) **ALLOW:** 3 hours

START

TIAN TAN BUDDHA (▷ 98–99)
🚇 Tung Chung and then buses or cable car for Po Lin

END

TUNG CHUNG
🚇 Tung Chung

1 From the bottom of the Big Buddha steps follow the sign for the Tea Garden. From there follow signs for the Wisdom Path. At a crossroads divert to the right to the Wisdom Path, a series of wooden obelisks marking out the infinity symbol.

2 Return to the crossroads and go straight across, following a fenced, level pathway through trees. Many of the plants growing here are labeled in Latin and English.

3 At the end of the path turn briefly on to a wide concrete path leading through a gateway decorated with calligraphy and pink knobs signposted to Tung Chung via Tei Tong Tsai.

4 The path winds downward through trees and ferns. About 0.6 miles (1km) from the gate, where the road forks, take a left along a concrete path past vegetable allotments.

8 From here you can take local bus 35 into Tung Chung town center.

7 The path follows a storm drain past derelict houses. The route crosses the storm drain and passes a secondary school on the left, arriving at Tung Chung Road. Turn left and 327 yards (300m) on the right is the entrance to Tung Chung Fort where the walk ends.

6 The path joins a concrete road. Turn right onto the road and find another concrete archway set into a wall on the left. Turn through the archway, passing beehives and banana trees. High-rise apartments are in view ahead.

5 Keep following signs to Tung Chung, passing Loh Hon Temple.

Excursions

GUANGZHOU

The capital of Guangdong province is both the crucible of Cantonese culture and China's historic economic powerhouse. Alongside Beijing and Shanghai, it's been at the forefront of China's modern transformation and the dynamism is palpable. Culture vultures will also find temples, colonial relics and the best restaurants in China.

Guangzhou makes for an interesting single or two-day trip from Hong Kong. Its history can be traced back to the third century BC when the area was settled by the armies of the first emperor, Qin Shi Huangdi. By the end of the first millennium AD, the city was an international port and it became one of the chief trading places as China opened up to overseas merchants from the 16th century.

Shamian Island is Guangzhou's most charming locale. Originally a sandbar on the Pearl River, the island was reclaimed and divided into foreign concessions after the Opium Wars of the mid-19th century. North of Shamian is the Qingping Market. Many stalls have moved inside in beautification and hygiene campaigns. Nevertheless, the area is charming for its old-world ambience and architecture.

In the east of the city is a brand new US-style gridded district studded with hotel towers, glass offices, a beautiful new opera house and the excellent Guangdong Museum. Across the river is the tallest structure in China, the 1,969ft (600m) Canton Tower. There's a tourist observation deck and a stomach-churning vertical drop ride on the tower's exterior.

THE BASICS

Distance: 75 miles (120km)
Journey Time: 2 hours (train) or 20 minutes (plane)
🚆 Express from Hung Hom: 12 trains run daily 7.25am–8.01pm
✈ From Chek Lap Kok
ℹ Yitai Square, Guangzhou

THE BASICS

Distance: 37 miles (60km)
Journey Time: 1 hour
by jetfoil 🚢 Jetfoil from
the Shun Tak Centre,
Connaught Road or China
Ferry Terminal, Canton
Road 🎫 Expensive
ℹ️ Largo do Senado,
Edificio Ritz No. 9, Macau
☎ 8397 1120. Hong Kong:
Shop 336, Shun Tak Centre,
200 Connaught Road,
Central ☎ 2857 2287
❓ Take your passport;
no visa required for North
Americans or Europeans
staying 20 days or less

MACAU

**People come to Macau for the cobbled
streets, baroque architecture and cuisine
of Portugal's last colony (surrendered in
1999). More people come to gamble in
the world's new casino capital.**

Macau is compact and most of the main places
of interest you can see in a day. Highlights
include the ruined facade of 17th-century
St. Paul's Church and the Jesuit Monte Fortress.
Hotels and good restaurants are easy to find,
and prices are agreeably lower than those
in Hong Kong. The things to buy here are
antiques, jewelry and electrical goods.
Rua de São Paulo has lots of antiques and
reproduction shops, as well as stores selling
Asian crafts. Largo de Senado has clothes shops
where there are good bargains in woolens.

THE BASICS

Distance: 25 miles (40km)
Journey Time: 40 min
🚇 MTR from Tsim TSha
Tsui East to border at Lo Wu
and Lok Ma Chau
❓ Visas must be obtained
in advance at travel agents
in Hong Kong. However,
visa regulations change so
please check before you
finalize your travel plans.
Single entry 5-day visas
are issued at the border
crossing for many Western
passport holders (NB: **not
available to US citizens**)

SHENZHEN

**Shenzhen is where China's capitalist
experiments were first made in
the 1980s. It is now China's richest
metropolis. Culture is at a premium but
there are also five US-style theme parks.**

Here you'll find Splendid China, a theme park
where the Great Wall, the Forbidden City
and the terra-cotta warriors, among other
monuments of Chinese art and architecture,
are reduced to one-fifteenth of their real size.
The China Folk Culture Village (opposite)
introduces the country's ethnic minorities.

The real draw here is the shopping—prices are
lower than in Hong Kong, though China's recent
economic boom has narrowed the price gap.

Shopping

LO WU COMMERCIAL CITY

Go no farther than the Chinese customs for this vast complex of shops selling, well, everything. Anything you saw and liked in Hong Kong, including last year's designer outfits at low, low prices, is probably here. Particularly good if you are considering some hand tailoring or want to buy some cloth to take home. Copies fill the shops. Take care of your personal property and bring toilet paper with you.
➕ Map ➤ 92–93 ✉ Lo

Wu 🚇 Lo Wu KCR
❓ Visas issued at border for many Western passport holders (NB: not US citizens)

NGONG PING VILLAGE

www.np360.com.hk
This village has been created as part of the Ngong Ping 360 tourism project and is designed to engender a sense of the original culture of this area. Right next to the Skyrail terminal, it is an ideal spot to pick up traditional and themed souvenirs.
➕ Map ➤ 92–93

✉ Lantau Island 🚇 Tung Chung, then Skyrail

THE SHOPPES

www.venetianmacau.com
Macau's Shoppes Venetian mall is a shopper's delight built around a "canal," and the place to go if you're looking for high-end luxury and designer goods.
➕ Map ➤ 92–93
✉ Macau 🚢 Jetfoil from Shun Tak Centre, Connaught Road or China Ferry Terminal, Canton Road ❓ Take your passport (➤ 104, Macau Basics panel)

Restaurants

PRICES

Prices are approximate, based on a 3-course meal for one person.
$$$ over HK$700
$$ HK$300–HK$700
$ under HK$300

360 BAR, RESTAURANT AND LOUNGE ($$$)

The views are top-notch, to say nothing of the wine list and decor at this chic venue, which majors on premium imported steaks. It's just a short stroll from the Hong Kong border in Shenzhen.
➕ Map ➤ 92–93

✉ Shangri-La Hotel, 1002 Jianshe Lu, Luohu, Shenzhen ☎ 755 8396 1380 🕐 Tue–Sat 6–11

ROBUCHON AU DOME ($$$)

www.grandlisboahotel.com/dining-roubochon_au_dome-en
Parisian favorite Joel Robuchon began working in Macau at Hotel Lisboa, winning three Michelin stars in the process. Those have been earned also in Lisboa's bigger, sister hotel. Given this is one of Asia's top eateries, the lunches are particularly good value.
➕ Off map ✉ 43rd floor, Hotel Grand Lisboa, Avenida

do Infante D. Henrique, Macau ☎ 853 8803 7878 🕐 Daily 12–2.30, 6.30–10.30 🚢 Macau Ferry

THE STOEP ($-$$)

www.stoep.com
This is a South African restaurant with an unlikely tropical charm. Sample South African *braai* and a bottle of Stellenbosch while gazing out at the lapping waves on one of Hong Kong's longest beaches, Cheung Sha.
➕ Map ➤ 92–93 ✉ 32 Lower Cheung Sha Village, Lantau Island ☎ 2980 2699 🕐 Daily 12–3, 6-10.30 🚢 Central Pier to Mui Wo

Half the fun of your stay in Hong Kong is finding and enjoying your hotel, whether it be five-star luxury or more basic accommodations, where you can meet other guests and exchange travelers' tales.

Where to Stay

Introduction

The Hong Kong hotel scene is divided between cheap rooms for budget-seeking travelers, and options for wealthy Chinese and the globetrotting foreign elite whose tariffs range from the very expensive to the eye-watering. Those looking for middle-of-the-road rooms in familiar branded hotels will find the city surprisingly expensive, but, if one is more adventurous, there are bargains to be had. Serious luxury is concentrated either side of Victoria Harbour while, as a rule, hotels become cheaper the farther north in Kowloon or the New Territories you are prepared to go.

Budget Hotels

Space is at a premium in Hong Kong so most rooms are likely to be smaller than you expect, even in luxury accommodations. The really budget places are guesthouses in Tsim Sha Tsui, in some of the very old apartment blocks. Be prepared for cramped rooms, little security and few facilities, but you get to stay right at the heart of the action for very little outlay. Walk around Tsim Sha Tsui with your backpack and the guesthouses will find you.

Online Reservations

Making reservations online can save you money, with some excellent last minute deals to be found. Fall (autumn) through to Chinese New Year sees reservations at their peak, and any major trade fairs in Hong Kong and Guangzhou also cause less availability and prices to spike. However, the heat of summer sees prices falling and the good deals on offer.

HOTEL TIPS

Check breakfast times before you make a reservation. Most hotels offer a bed-and-breakfast rate and the better ones could fill you up for the day. Places that offer late breakfast (say until 11am) are worth seeking out, especially if you are a night bird. If you are staying in a budget place, bring your own padlock. Some places offer lockers to store your things.

Budget Hotels

PRICES

Expect to pay between HK$300 and HK$700 per night for a budget hotel.

ALISAN GUEST HOUSE

http://home.hkstar.com/alisangh

These 30 rooms are on the fifth floor of a block in Causeway Bay. All rooms have showers, lavatories and air-conditioning. Friendly owners.

G10 Flat A, 5th floor, Hoito Court, 275 Gloucester Road, Causeway Bay 2838 0762 Causeway Bay

BISHOP LEI INTERNATIONAL HOUSE

www.bishopleihtl.com.hk

At the upper end of the budget spectrum, Bishop Lei is a friendly, business-like hotel and has a great Mid-Levels location. Standard and double rooms go for around HK$700.

C10 4 Robinson Road, Mid Levels, Central 2868 0828 Central then Mid-Levels Escalator

CARITAS BIANCHI LODGE

www.caritas-chs.org.hk

Tidy, clean and well-run accommodations. The laundry and the restaurant are the only facilities.

F5 4 Cliff Road, Yau Ma Tei 2388 1111 Yau Ma Tei

CARITAS LODGE (BOUNDARY STREET)

www.caritas-chs.org.hk

Good accommodations—basic and roomy with a coffee shop, laundry facilities and spa.

G3 134 Boundary Street, Kowloon 2339 3777 Prince Edward, then bus 2D

GUANGZHOU GUESTHOUSE

A guesthouse in the Mirador Mansion that feels slightly removed from backpacker conditions. It's very simple, and rooms are very small. But with air-conditioned, ensuite singles going for HK$150 its rooms are good value.

F7 Flat B1/10F, Mirador Mansion, 54–64 Nathan Road, Tsim Sha Tsui 2311 2005 Tsim Sha Tsui

CHUNGKING MANSIONS

For so many years a must for budget travelers, Chungking Mansions in Tsim Sha Tsui may just have reached its sell-by date. Still the cheapest place to stay in Hong Kong, the disadvantages of the cramped, inadequate elevators and heavily populated staircases outweigh the financial savings. Lots of the accommodations now cater to long-stay immigrant workers and the backpackers who wander in there look a little frazzled.

HONG KONG HOSTEL

www.hostel.hk

The best value for budget accommodations on the island. A series of rooms in a block of apartments, most with private bath, phone, fridge and TV. Communal kitchen.

H10 Flat A2, 3rd floor, Paterson Building, 47 Paterson Street, Causeway Bay 2392 6868 Causeway Bay

NEW GARDEN HOSTEL

Mirador Mansions is fast becoming the new Chungking Mansions—a great place for meeting other backpackers and swapping stories. There's a choice of shower or bath and an open terrace. One of several hostels sharing the building.

F7 Flat 1 E1, 13th Floor, Mirador Mansion, 58–62 Nathan Road, Tsim Sha Tsui 2311 2523 Tsim Sha Tsui

RENT A ROOM

www.rentaroomhk.com

A businesslike place with air-conditioning, fridge, rooms with private bathrooms and some with a kitchenette. Book a dorm room with a shared bathroom for an even more economical stay. In a nice area at the top of the Golden Mile.

F6 7–8 Tak Hing Street, Knight Garden Flat A, 2nd floor, Jordan 2366 3011 Jordan

Mid-Range Hotels

PRICES

Expect to pay between HK$700 and HK$2,000 per night for a mid-range hotel.

EATON

www.eaton-hotel.com
Large, with a range of room rates, as well as restaurants, swimming pool, gym and a bar. Catch any bus stopping outside the door to get to Tsim Sha Tsui. Rates fall dramatically 24–48 hours before you plan to arrive.
🔲 F6 ✉ 380 Nathan Road, Yau Ma Tei ☎ 2782 1818
🚇 Jordan

THE EXCELSIOR

www.mandarinoriental.com/excelsior
Pleasant and casual with nice rooms and a huge range of facilities, right down to the two covered tennis courts on the roof. Convenient for shopping and nightlife.
🔲 G10 ✉ 281 Gloucester Road, Causeway Bay ☎ 2894 8888 🚇 Causeway Bay

THE MIRA HOTEL

www.themirahotel.com
This once achingly average hotel is now chic and boutiquey, and has a good spa and a choice of restaurants. The Mira is also in a great location, right opposite Kowloon Park.
🔲 F7 ✉ 118 Nathan Road, Tsim Sha Tsui ☎ 2368 1111
🚇 Tsim Sha Tsui

HOTEL PANORAMA

www.hotelpanorama.com.hk
This hotel is in a high-rise in the thick of Tsim Sha Tsui. The design is slick and contemporary, with lots of dark wood and mirrors. There are wide harbor views, interrupted only by a couple of new tower blocks. The top floor restaurant and bar are outstanding.
🔲 F7 ✉ 8A Hart Avenue, Tsim Sha Tsui ☎ 3550 0388
🚇 Tsim Sha Tsui

KOWLOON HOTEL

www.harbour-plaza.com/klnh
This is a modern place with many facilities but tiny rooms. However, each room has its own internet connection, while some have harbor views. Breakfast is not included in rate.
🔲 F8 ✉ 19–21 Nathan Road, Tsim Sha Tsui ☎ 2929 2888 🚇 Tsim Sha Tsui

CAMPING

There are lots of places to camp in the SAR, especially in the country parks and on some of the outlying islands. The Agriculture, Fisheries and Conservation department lists 41 campsites in the country parks, most very basic with toilet facilities, a water supply and little more. They are mostly intended as stopping points on walks. You must bring your own equipment and, in the dry season, your own water.

LAN KWAI FONG HOTEL

www.lankwaifonghotel.com.hk
Great location and excellent value at this boutique hotel with oriental decor and lots of facilities, including a gym and WiFi. The suites are a bit more expensive but have great views over the city. The homey atmosphere here gives it an advantage over some of the 5-star hotels.
🔲 C9 ✉ 3 Kau U Fong, Central ☎ 3650 0000
🚇 Central

GLOUCESTER LUK KWOK

www.gloucesterlukkwok.com.hk
This is really a business-oriented hotel but it's good value for money and central. The rooms are small and all on the floors above the 19th. Two restaurants and a private cocktail bar for guests. No-smoking rooms also.
🔲 F10 ✉ 72 Gloucester Road, Wan Chai ☎ 2866 2166 🚇 Wan Chai

THE LUXE MANOR

www.theluxemanor.com
A boutique hotel with a difference near Knutsford Terrace. From the giant wooden swing doors of the lobby, to the scarlet bins in the rooms, it oozes glamor. One for the bohemian, or fashionista.
🔲 F7 ✉ 39 Kimberley Road, Tsim Sha Tsui ☎ 3763 8888
🚇 Tsim Sha Tsui

MINGLE PLACE

www.mingleplace.com
This likeable hotel makes the traditionally tiny rooms of Kowloon seem that much bigger through a slick combination of glass, mirrors and light wood. The Temple Street night market is close by.
✚ F7 ✉ 8 Observatory Court, Tsim Sha Tsui
☎ 2377 1180

NATHAN HOTEL

www.nathanhotel.com
Big rooms in this small and quiet place close to Jordan MRT. Well run, with everything you need to get by, including a babysitting service.
✚ F6 ✉ 378 Nathan Road, Tsim Sha Tsui ☎ 2388 5141
🚇 Jordan

NEWTON

www.newtonhk.com
A little way out but you get a good hotel with a Shanghainese restaurant, close to the MRT with a shuttle service to the airport, an outdoor pool and internet. Small but well- appointed rooms.
✚ J9 ✉ 218 Electric Road, North Point ☎ 2807 2333
🚇 Fortress Hill

PRUDENTIAL HOTEL

www.prudentialhotel.com
A little out of the way but it has all the facilities that a 3-star hotel demands, with a swimming pool on the roof.
✚ F7 ✉ 222 Nathan Road, Tsim Sha Tsui ☎ 2311 8222
🚇 Jordan

ROSEDALE

www.rosedalehotels.com.hk
This is a relatively new hotel, in Causeway Bay and close to the shops. All the usual facilities in the room plus a massage service, fitness room, wireless broadband and no-smoking rooms.
✚ H10 ✉ 8 Shelter Street, Causeway Bay ☎ 2127 8888
🚇 Causeway Bay

ROYAL PARK

www.royalpark.com.hk
Big rooms and good facilities, including a pool and a free shuttle bus into town. If you don't mind the half-hour ride into town each day, this is great value and it's close to some of the excellent walks and parks of the New Territories.
✚ Map ▷ 92–93
✉ 8 Pak Hok Ting Street, Sha Tin ☎ 2601 2111
🚇 Sha Tin MTR

CHOOSING YOUR HOTEL

Choosing a good place to stay among the hundreds of accommodations available in this vibrant city can prove to be a really tricky business. Before you book your hotel, you may care to look at a few websites to get an idea of what is available within your desired location and price range. There can be some excellent bargains online if you are prepared to leave it to the last minute.

ROYAL PLAZA

www.royalplaza.com.hk
A little way out of the center in Mong Kok this hotel is close to some great bargain shopping places and markets. The hotel's rather bland rooms are compensated for the lower prices that staying out of the center brings. Good Chinese restaurant and an all-day buffet in the Western restaurant. Also a gym, sauna and swimming pool.
✚ F3 ✉ 193 Prince Edward Road West, Mong Kok
☎ 2928 8822
🚇 Mong Kok MTR

THE SALISBURY

www.ymcahk.org.hk
This 366-room YMCA is convenient for the shops and the Star Ferry. It has an inexpensive self-service restaurant and offers free use of a swimming pool. There are some harbor-view rooms.
✚ F8 ✉ 41 Salisbury Road, Tsim Sha Tsui
☎ 2268 7888
🚇 Tsim Sha Tsui

STANFORD HILLVIEW

www.stanfordhillview.com
The Stanford Hillview is a small, quiet hotel near the Knutsford Terrace nightspot. It offers a gym, room, wireless broadband and a bar. There is a shuttle service to the airport train.
✚ F7 ✉ 13–17 Observatory Road, Tsim Sha Tsui ☎ 2722 7822 🚇 Tsim Sha Tsui

Luxury Hotels

PRICES

Expect to pay more than HK$2,000 per night for a luxury hotel.

THE FOUR SEASONS

www.fourseasons.com/hongkong

Beautifully designed with loving attention to detail, the Four Seasons offers guests the utmost in comfort. Restaurants, bars and a stunning rooftop swimming pool with underwater music.

➕ C9 ✉ 8 Finance Street ☎ 3196 8888 🚇 Central

GRAND HYATT, WAN CHAI

www.hongkong.grand.hyatt.com

With amazing city views and large rooms, the Grand Hyatt promises an enjoyable stay. Friendly staff tend to your every need and the bars and restaurants may mean you never have to leave the hotel.

➕ F10 ✉ 1 Harbour Road ☎ 2588 1234 🚇 Wan Chai

INTERCONTINENTAL HONG KONG

www.hongkong-ic.intercontinental.com

Simple, elegant hotel, with good *feng shui* and some of the best views of the island across the harbor. Great swimming pool. Award-winning Cantonese restaurant.

➕ F8 ✉ 18 Salisbury Road, Tsim Sha Tsui ☎ 2721 1211 🚇 Tsim Sha Tsui

ISLAND SHANGRI-LA

www.shangri-la.com

Towering above Central with amazing views over the city this luxurious hotel has spacious, well-designed rooms, some great places to eat and drink, and the world's longest Chinese painting. Good fitness suite and pool. Library for guests.

➕ E11 ✉ Pacific Place, Supreme Court Road, Central ☎ 2877 3838 🚇 Central

LANGHAM PLACE HOTEL

http://hongkong.langham-placehotels.com

The only 5-star hotel in Mong Kok, Langham Place has an impressive line-up of guest facilities with flat-screen TVs, huge rooms with enormous marble tile bathrooms, great service from a dedicated staff

ISLAND OR KOWLOON?

If you are staying at one of For top-drawer hotels in Hong Kong you should decide whether you want to stay on the island or in Kowloon. Some of the hotel chains, such as Shangri-La, have hotels in both areas and most of them have amazing views across the harbor. If you love to stay in your room, then Kowloon has better views of the nightly Symphony of Lights but if you're a nightlife lover then the island is the place for you.

and, best of all, a really good spa complete with private treatment rooms and all kinds of health and beauty treatments.

➕ E4 ✉ 555 Shanghai Street, Mong Kok ☎ 3552 3388 🚇 Mong Kok

MANDARIN ORIENTAL

www.mandarinoriental.com/hongkong

The very central Mandarin Oriental has a long tradition of impeccable service. Well-appointed rooms, with attention to detail, helpful staff, classy shops, great pool, excellent restaurants. It has reopened after a huge refit and is looking better than ever.

➕ D10 ✉ 5 Connaught Road, Central ☎ 2522 0111 🚇 Central

RITZ-CARLTON HONG KONG

www.ritzcarlton.com/hongkong

Sumptuous new hotel lodged in the uppermost floors of one of Hong Kong's tallest buildings. There are two Michelin Star-winning restaurants, the world's highest bar (▷ 73) and a spectacular spa-with-a-view. Rooms have 42-inch TVs as standard, and imposing marble bathrooms. A splurge option.

➕ D6 ✉ 103rd–118th floor, International Commerce Centre, 1 Austin Road West, Kowloon ☎ 2263 2263 🚇 Kowloon

By contrast, we close

This section offers all you need to know
about Hong Kong, from how to pay your
tram fare to where to go to send an email,
to opening hours and health precautions—
all the ins and outs of a visit.

Need to Know

Planning Ahead

When to Go

The ideal time to visit is between October and mid-December, when the days are warm and fresh and the nights are cool. Try to avoid June through September, when the weather is extremely hot and humid. The hotels are at their most expensive from late fall to early February.

TIME

Hong Kong is 8 hours ahead of the UK, 13 hours ahead of New York and 16 hours ahead of Los Angeles.

AVERAGE DAILY MAXIMUM TEMPERATURES											
JAN	FEB	MAR	APR	MAY	JUN	JUL	AUG	SEP	OCT	NOV	DEC
64°F	63°F	66°F	75°F	82°F	84°F	88°F	88°F	84°F	81°F	73°F	68°F
18°C	17°C	19°C	24°C	28°C	29°C	31°C	31°C	29°C	27°C	23°C	20°C

Spring (March through May) is usually warm, although rain is common.
Summer (June through September) is very hot and humid, with nearly 16in (400mm) of rain on average each month. The clammy heat sometimes gives way to violent typhoons.
Fall (October through to mid-December) is usually warm.
Winter (mid-December through February) is comfortable, with occasional cold spells.
Typhoons hit between July and September. Hotels post the appropriate storm signal: Storm Signal 1=Typhoon within 500 miles (800km) of Hong Kong; Storm Signal 3=Typhoon on its way, be prepared; Storm Signal 8=Stay in your hotel, dangerous winds with gusts.

WHAT'S ON

January/February *Chinese (Lunar) New Year*: This event looms large in Hong Kong life. The week before the New Year is busy; the harbor fireworks display is magnificent, but the crowds are enormous.

Mid-February/mid-March *Arts Festival*: International orchestral, dance and theater events over four weeks.

March *Hong Kong Sevens*: This rugby tournament is a wild three-day-long expat party.

Late March/April *International Film Festival*: For two weeks; various venues.

April *Ching Ming*: Tomb-sweeping day.

Tin Hau Festival: Tin Hau temples remember a 12th-century legend about a girl who saves her brother from drowning. Fishing junks and temples are decorated and Chinese street operas held near the temples.

Birthday of Lord Buddha (late April): At temples Buddha's statue is ceremonially bathed, symbolically washing away sins and material encumbrances.

May/June *Dragon Boat Festival*: Noisy, dragon-boat races are enthusiastically held to commemorate the political protests of a 4th-century poet and patriot, Chu Yuan.

August/September *Hungry Ghosts Festival*: Offerings of food are set out to placate roaming spirits in this traditional Buddhist festival.

September/October *Mid-Autumn Festival*: Families head out with lanterns and eat mooncakes to commemorate the fullest moon of the year.

Hong Kong Online

www.discoverhongkong.com
The official website of the Hong Kong Tourist
Board. General information about Hong Kong,
suggestions for day trips, family days out,
history, information on transport, etc.

www.timeout.com.hk
The website of the magazine of the same
name. Lots of information on what's on,
restaurant reviews and shopping tips, all aimed
at a young audience.

www.gayhk.com
Information about Hong Kong's gay scene,
attitudes in the territory, good places to visit,
reviews of clubs, bars and more.

www.scmp.com
This is the site of the *South China Morning
Post,* the territory's independent newspaper.
News items, cultural information, current affairs.
(A few articles are free then paywalled.)

www.thestandard.com.hk
Breaking news from Hong Kong's second
English-language newspaper. Unlike rival SCMP
(above), all content can be accessed for free.

www.skybird.com.hk
Information and prices for tours of this accredited travel agency in the city.

www.grayline.com.hk
A well-established tour company gives details
of tours of the island and trips into China.

www.hongkongairport.com
The site of Hong Kong International Airport
provides useful information before you arrive.

www.hkclubbing.com
This site keeps track of the new and not so new
clubs in the city.

USEFUL WEBSITES

www.fodors.com
A complete travel-planning
site. You can research prices
and weather, reserve air
tickets, cars and rooms, ask
questions (and get answers)
from fellow visitors, and find
links to other sites.

www.mtr.com.hk
Information on the metro
system in Hong Kong. Details
of Octopus cards, airport
express, tourist passes, and
many other useful details.

www.tripadvisor.com
Website selling hotel deals,
which has reviews by
visitors, many of them
very candid.

INTERNET CAFÉS

Hong Kong Central Library
🚇 H9   ✉ 66 Causeway
Road, Causeway Bay
☎ 3150 1234   🕐 Thu–Tue
10–9, Wed 1–9   💷 Free

Pacific Coffee Company
This mega-chain has outlets
across the SAR.
🚇 F7   ✉ Miramar
Shopping Centre G31–32A,
132 Nathan Road, Tsim
Sha Tsui   ☎ 2735 0112
🕐 Mon–Thu 7am–midnight,
Fri, Sat 7am–1am, Sun
8am–midnight   💷 Free with
purchase of coffee

Getting There

ENTRY REQUIREMENTS

All visitors must hold a valid passport. For the latest passport and visa information, look at website www.immd.gov.hk

VISITORS WITH DISABILITIES

Generally speaking wheel-chair users will find that the newer buildings have good access while older buildings and most streets, MTR stations, footbridges (of which there are hundreds), and shopping centers are difficult to negotiate. Taxis, ferries and some buses are wheelchair friendly.

Joint Council for the Physically and Mentally Disabled

🏢 11th–13th floor, Duke of Windsor Social Services Building, 15 Hennessy Road, Wan Chai ☎ 2864 2929, www.hkcss.org.hk

AIRPORTS

All flights land at Hong Kong International Airport at Chek Lap Kok, 15 miles (24km) west of Hong Kong city. The eight floors of the airport include three banks, a moneychanger, several ATMs, a tourist information office and acres of restaurants and bars.

18 miles (30km) 12 miles (20km) 6 miles (10km)

❎ **Chek Lap Kok Airport** ● **Hong Kong**

ARRIVING AT CHEK LAP KOK AIRPORT

For airport information ☎ 2181 0000; www.hongkongairport.com.

The Airport Express (☎ 2881 8888; www.mtr.com.hk) is the most efficient and pleasant way of getting to town from the airport. Trains depart for the city at 12-minute intervals from 5.40am to 12.48am; journey time to Central is 24 minutes, to Kowloon 18 minutes; cost HK$100 one way to/from Central, HK$90 to/from Kowloon, with a return fare costing HK$180 and HK$160 respectively.

There are also bus services into Hong Kong Island, Kowloon, the New Territories and Lantau Island, which are less expensive. Information on times and prices can be obtained from the tourist office in the airport or www.citybus. com.hk. The Citybus A11 travels into Hong Kong Island for HK$40, while the A21 serves Kowloon for HK$33.

A taxi to Hong Kong Island is the expensive option and will cost around HK$340. This includes the toll fare for the Lantau Link, the bridge that joins Lantau Island to Hong Kong Island. The journey to Kowloon costs around HK$270.

ARRIVING BY BUS

Bus services from Shenzhen and a host of Pearl River Delta (Guangdong) cities are provided by CTS Express coaches. There are buses to downtown stops and direct buses to the airport. ✉ Room 209 KCRC Hung Hom Building, 8 Cheong Wan Road, Hung Hom ☎ 2764 9803. To travel into China you must get a visa in advance of your journey.

ARRIVING BY TRAIN

High-speed trains travel from Guangzhou East railway station to Hung Hom 12 times a day 8.19am–9.32pm. There are also rail links with Shanghai and Beijing.

EMBASSIES AND CONSULATES

● **Australia** ✉ 23rd and 24th Floors, Harbour Centre, 25 Harbour Road, Wan Chai ☎ 2827 8881

● **Canada** ✉ 12th–14th floors, One Exchange Square, 8 Connaught Place, Central ☎ 3719 4700

● **Germany** ✉ 21st floor, United Centre, 95 Queensway, Central ☎ 2105 8788

● **UK** ✉ 1 Supreme Court Road, Admiralty ☎ 2901 3000

● **US** ✉ 26 Garden Road, Central ☎ 2523 9011

Getting Around

- Hong Kong is very crowded, night and day, and professional thieves capitalize on this.
- Keep wallets and purses secure.
- Keep traveler's checks separate from the invoice that lists their numbers.
- Don't leave valuables where you can't see them at all times.
- Keep travel documents and money in a hotel safe.

Lost Property
- ✉ Admiralty MTR station
- 🕐 Mon–Sat 8–7
- ☎ 2861 0020

TOURIST INFORMATION

- The Hong Kong Tourist Board (HKTB) has two downtown offices:
✉ Star Ferry Concourse, Tsim Sha Tsui 🕐 Daily 8–8 ✉ Causeway Bay MTR 🕐 Daily 8–8

- Visitor Hotline:
☎ 2508 1234, daily 8–6
- The tourist board has developed the Quality Tourism Services scheme. Look for the QTS logo.

SKYRAIL

Skyrail is an aerial cable car linking Tung Chung with Ngong Ping on Lantau Island.

TRAINS

- The MTR (Mass Transit Railway) is the quickest way to hop between shopping areas on Hong Kong Island, TST and the New Territories.
- Stations have clear instructions in both English and Chinese for operating ticket machines. Machines issue thin plastic cards that are also available from information/ticket counters. Fares are between HK$4.5 and HK$5.5. Tickets have a magnetic strip and the fare is deducted automatically as you pass through the ticket barrier ☎ 2881 8888.
- MTR maps are available at the airport and can be found in most hotel lobbies. MTR stations dispense a free guide to the system in English and Chinese.

BUSES

Traveling on buses is not really recommended (except for trips to the south side of Hong Kong Island), but in the event of using one, note the fixed fare is marked on the bus as you enter and pay; no change is given. The MTR train network is faster and easier to use. Tourist Board offices have a free map showing bus fares and routes.

TAXIS

Taxis are good value and can be picked up at ranks, although many drivers do not speak English. Once inside you must use the seat belt.
- The flagfare for red "downtown" taxis is HK$18, and after a 1.5-mile (2km) distance the fare increases by HK$1.40 for every 210 yards (200m). There is a HK$5 additional charge if a taxi is reserved by phone and comes to your pick-up point. An additional charge of HK$5 may be made for each large piece of baggage. Fares might be slightly different in the New Territories and Lantau.
- A "For Hire" sign is displayed in the windscreen; at night a "Taxi" sign is lit up on the roof.
- Taxis are not supposed to stop at bus stops or on a yellow line.

TRAMS

● Trams run only on Hong Kong's north side—the route between Kennedy Town in the west and Causeway Bay in the east is one of the most useful.

● Destinations are marked on the front in English.

● The fixed fare of HK$2 is dropped in the paybox before leaving the tram.

THE OCTOPUS CARD

If you are planning to stay in Hong Kong for any length of time, you might want to consider buying an Octopus Card (HK$150). This is a prepaid card that can be used on most of the city's transport systems, but is also starting to come into use in shops and other businesses to replace cash. The card is not personalized in any way and the HK$100 deposit required is refundable. The drawback to the card of course is that it operates in the same way as cash so if lost or misplaced the cash value is also lost. You can check the balance of cash remaining on the ticket each time you use it.

ORGANIZED SIGHTSEEING

● The **Hong Kong Tourist Board** (▷ 118) conducts tours to a number of destinations, as well as lots of theme tours.

● **Splendid** organizes personalized tours of Hong Kong and South China, including an Aberdeen or harbor night cruise, horse racing (June–September), Lantau Island and a Splendid Night of Delight, as well as tours into China (☎ 2316 2151; www.splendidtours.com ● **Water Tours Ltd.** conducts nearly 20 different harbor cruises, including a Sampan ride around Aberdeen (☎ 2926 3868; www.watertours.com.hk).

● **Star Ferry** runs ten harbor tours a day (☎ 2366 7024; www.starferry.com.hk).

● **Grayline Tours** offers city tours, dinner cruises and day trips to China (☎ 23168 7111; www.grayline.com.hk).

LONE TRAVELERS

● Hong Kong is similar to, and often safer than, European or North American cities; take common-sense precautions.

● Public transportation at night is as safe as during the day.

STUDENT TRAVELERS

● There are few discounts for ISIC (International Student Identity Card) holders.

● The Student Travel Bureau dispenses a free booklet detailing retail outlets with student discounts ⊠ Room 1021, 10/F, Star House, Tsim Sha Tsui ☎ 2730 3269 ⏰ 9.30–6

● Some places of interest have a reduced student admission price.

EMERGENCY NUMBERS

Police/Fire/Ambulance
☎ 999

THE MID LEVELS

Special to Hong Kong is the 15-minute trip up to the Mid Levels on escalators. The series of escalators begins in Central, on Des Voeux Road, and extends up through the residential tiers in hilly Central (▷ 31).

Essential Facts

- Offices: Mon–Fri 9–5, Sat 9–1.
- Banks: Mon–Fri 9–4.30, Sat 9–12.30.
- Post offices: Mon–Fri 9.30–5, Sat 9.30–1.
- Shops: Daily 10–6, often 10–9/11–11 in tourist areas.

MONEY

The unit of currency is the Hong Kong dollar (= 100 cents). Notes comes in denominations of 10, 20, 50, 100, 500 and 1,000; coins are 10, 20 and 50 cents.

ETIQUETTE

- Shaking hands is common practice, as is the exchanging of business cards, presented with both hands.
- Don't be surprised when people push, shove and jump the line or fail to line up at all.
- A service charge is usually added to restaurant bills, but the staff do not get this money as tips so an extra 10 percent is expected. Round up taxi fares to the next dollar or two.

MEDICAL TREATMENT

- Outpatient departments of public or private hospitals provide emergency treatment.
- Private doctors (see Yellow Pages) charge HK$150 per visit on average. This usually includes three days' medication.
- **Public hospitals:**

Queen Mary Hospital ✉ 102 Pok Fu Lam Road, Hong Kong Island ☎ 2855 3838

Queen Elizabeth Hospital ✉ 30 Gascoigne Road, Kowloon ☎ 2958 8888

Kwong Wah Hospital ✉ 25 Waterloo Road, Yau Ma Tei, Kowloon ☎ 2332 2311

- **Private hospitals:**

Adventist ✉ 40 Stubbs Road, Wan Chai, Hong Kong Island ☎ 2574 6211

Baptist ✉ 222 Waterloo Road, Kowloon Tong ☎ 2339 8888

MONEY MATTERS

- Traveler's checks can often be used as payment or cashed at banks or money-changers. Always check the exchange rate before making any transaction; banks offer the best rates. There are scores of small streetside money-changers (particularly in Tsim Sha Tsui and Causesway Bay). It's safe to change cash here, though shop around for the best deal as rates vary.
- Credit cards—Visa, Access (MasterCard), American Express and Diners Club—are widely accepted for purchases in shops and restaurants. In small shops check commission is not added—this is illegal.

● Credit cards can be used to obtain cash from banks and ATM machines. Some Hong Kong Bank teller machines provide 24-hour HK$ withdrawal facilities for Visa and MasterCard holders. Amex holders have the same facility at some Jetco ATMs, as well as the Express ATMs.

NATIONAL HOLIDAYS
Dates of the Chinese lunar festivals vary from year to year.
● 1 January: New Year's Day.
● Late January or early February: Chinese New Year (three days).
● Good Friday and Easter Monday.
● Early April: Ching Ming Festival.
● 4 April/early May: Buddha's birthday.
● 1 May: Labor Day.
● Mid- to late-June: Dragon Boat Festival.
● 1 July: Hong Kong SAR Establishment Day.
● Late September or early October: Mid-Autumn Festival.
● 1 October: China National Day.
● Mid- to late October: Cheung Yeung Festival.
● 25 and 26 December: Christmas Day and Boxing Day.

NEWSPAPERS, MAGAZINES, TV AND RADIO
● International newspapers and magazines are available in bookstores, newsagents and hotel kiosks. The newsagent at the Star Ferry terminal in Tsim Sha Tsui and the bookstore at the ferry terminal in Central have a good selection.
● There are two English-language daily newspapers: the broadsheet *South China Morning Post* and the tabloid *Hong Kong Standard*.
● For entertainment listings look for the free, bi-weekly *HK Magazine* or the paid-for *Time Out Hong Kong*.
● The two main TV stations, TVB and ATV, each has one channel broadcast mainly in English—TVB Pearl and ATV World—though Mandarin and Cantonese are interspersed.
● Public radio broadcaster RTHK has only one English language channel, but does provide a live feed of the UK's BBC World Service.

TOILETS
● Most are Western style.
● Hotels are the best places to find clean toilets.
● Public toilets are free.
● Always carry a packet of tissues.

ELECTRICITY

● The current is 200/220 volts, 50 cycles alternating current (AC).

● Most wall outlets take three square prongs; some older ones take three large round prongs.

● US appliances require a converter and a plug adaptor.

PLACES OF WORSHIP

● **Protestant Evangelical Community Church** ✉ 4th floor YMCA, Salisbury Road, Tsim Sha Tsui ☎ 2369 2211

● **The Roman Catholic Cathedral** ✉ 16 Cairn Road, Mid Levels, Hong Kong Island ☎ 2810 4066

● **Jewish Ohel Leah Synagogue** ✉ 70 Robinson Road, Central ☎ 2857 6095

● **Kowloon Mosque** ✉ Kowloon Park ☎ 2724 0095

POST OFFICES

The General Post Office on Hong Kong Island is at 2 Connaught Place, Central.

● In Kowloon, the main post office is at the ground floor of the Kowloon Government Offices, 405 Nathan Road, Yau Ma Tei.

● Letters and postcards to destinations outside Southeast Asia cost HK$3.60 for up to 30g.

● The Speedpost service (☎ 2921 2277) cuts the usual five-day service to Europe or North America by about half.

TELEPHONES

● Local calls are free from private homes. Public phones charge HK$1 per call and sometimes only take HK$2 coins without giving change. Pressing the "FC" (follow-on call) button before hanging up allows a second call.

● Phonecards, available in denominations of HK$50 and HK$100 at 7–Eleven stores and other shops, are easier to use, especially for International Direct Dialling calls.

● Some telephone boxes accept only phonecards or only coins.

● For IDD calls, dial 001, followed by the country code and then the area code (minus any initial 0) and number. Dial 013 for information about international calls.

● To call Hong Kong from abroad dial 00 852, then the 8-digit number.

Language

Hong Kong has two official languages: Chinese and English. While English is spoken widely in business circles and tourist areas, it is not always understood elsewhere. It's best to get the hotel receptionist to write down your destination in Chinese. A few words of Cantonese, the main Chinese dialect, will go a long way in establishing rapport—and off the beaten track they may prove very useful.

BASICS

neih wuih mwuih gong ying mahn?	Can you speak English?
jóu sahn	Good morning
néih hou ma?	How are you?
wai! (pronounced 'why')	Hello (only on the phone)
mgòi	Thank you (for a favor)
dò jeh	Thank you (for a gift)
mgòi	Please
mgòi	Excuse me
deui mjyuh	I'm sorry
haih or hou	yes
mhaih or mhou	no
bin douh?	where?
fèi gèi chèung	airport
bā si	bus
dihn chè	tram
géi dô?	How many/how much?
géi dō chin?	How much is it?
géi dim jung?	What time is it?

NUMBERS

leng	0
yāt	1
yih	2
sàam	3
sei	4
ngh	5
luhk	6
chát	7
baat	8
gáu	9
sahp	10
sahp yāt	11
yih sahp	20
yih sahp yāt	21
saam sahp	30
sei sahp	40
ngh sahp	50
luhk sahp	60
chát sahp	70
baat sahp	80
gáu sahp	90
gáu sahp gáu	99
yāt baak	100
yāt chihn	1000

Timeline

WORLD WAR II

In 1937, hundreds of thousands of Chinese, displaced by the Japanese invasion of China, sought refuge in Hong Kong. On December 8, 1941, Japanese aircraft bombed Kowloon, and by Christmas Day the British had surrendered. More than 2,000 people died and 10,000 soldiers were taken prisoner. British civilians were incarcerated in Stanley Prison. With the surrender of the Japanese in August 1945, Hong Kong again became a British colony.

4000BC Early settlement left some pottery, stone tools and iron implements—then for many centuries the islands had more pirates than farmers.

c200BC The Chinese Empire is unified and for the next millennium-and-a-half Hong Kong Island is ruled by a governor based in Canton.

1685 British and French merchants begin to deal in tea and silk. The British later start to import opium as a way of extending their power and profits.

1839–42 Chinese attempts to block the import of opium end in defeat; the treaty concluding the first Opium War cedes Hong Kong Island to the British "in perpetuity." Within two decades, another treaty concedes the Kowloon Peninsula. In 1889 a further treaty leases substantial land north of Kowloon—the New Territories—to Britain for 99 years.

1941–45 Japanese occupation (▷ panel, this page).

1949 The Communist victory in China leads to refugee influxes.

1950–53 When the US imposes sanctions against China during the Korean War the colony develops a manufacturing base of its own.

Murray House, a former government building; an old post box; Lei Cheng Uk Museum; a flag-raising ceremony; Golden Bauhina next to Hong Kong Convention Centre (left to right)

NEED TO KNOW   TIMELINE

1967 The political passions rocking China spill over into Hong Kong, with riots and strikes. The colony seems on the brink of a premature closure of its lease, but normality soon returns.

1975 100,000 Vietnamese refugees arrive.

1982 British Prime Minister Margaret Thatcher goes to Beijing to discuss the colony's future.

1984 The Sino-British Joint Declaration confirms the return of the colony to China. In 1988 Beijing publishes its Basic Law for Hong Kong citizens, guaranteeing their rights.

1989 The Tiananmen Square massacre confirms Hong Kong's fears about its future under China's sovereignty. A million people protest on the streets of Hong Kong.

1997 Hong Kong becomes a Special Administrative Region of China. English remains an official language. People from other parts of China require special approval for entry.

2003 SARS epidemic hits Hong Kong.

2007 Tenth anniversary of the Handover.

2014 Controversy over democratic reform intensifies. On July 1, more than 100,000 people take to the streets calling for greater freedom to choose Hong Kong's top official.

THE HANDOVER

At midnight on June 30, 1997, Britain's last vestige of empire was handed back to the Chinese. Trepidation surrounded the occasion, but in the event it was a muted affair in one of the worst rainstorms in memory. Few people were on the streets. Chris Patten, Hong Kong's last governor, and Prince Charles quietly and tearfully slipped away on the royal yacht *Britannia* and the Red Army silently drove across the border. The expatriate workers who had not chosen to leave marked the occasion in Lan Kwai Fong bars, and everyone woke up the next day a little nervously, wondering how their lives would be changed, and a little shocked that nothing seemed different.

Index

Published by AA Publishing, a trading name of AA Media Limited, whose
registered office is Fanum House, Basing View, Basingstoke, Hampshire
RG21 4EA. Registered number 06112600.

WRITTEN BY Joseph Levy Sheehan
ADDITIONAL TEXT AND UPDATED BY Graham Bond
SERIES EDITOR Clare Ashton
DESIGN WORK Tracey Freestone
IMAGE RETOUCHING AND REPRO Ian Little

Colour separation by AA Digital Department
Printed and bound by Leo Paper Products, China

A CIP catalogue record for this book is available from the British Library.

ISBN 978-0-7495-7800-8

A05378
Maps in this title produced from mapping © MAIRDUMONT / Falk Verlag 2013
and data from openstreetmap.org
© OpenStreetMap contributors
Transport map © Communicarta Ltd, UK

The Automobile Association would like to thank the following photographers, companies and picture libraries for their assistance in the preparation of this book.

2-18 AA/B Bachman; **4tl** AA/B Bachman; **5** AA/B Bachman; **6cl** AA/B Bachman; **6c** AA/N Hicks; **6cr** AA/B Bachman; **6bl** AA/B Bachman; **6bc** AA/B Bachman; **6br** AA Photodisc; **7tl** AA/B Bachman; **7tcl** AA/B Bachman; **7tcr** Courtesy of Hong Kong Tourism Board; **7tr** Courtesy of Hong Kong Tourism Board; **7cl** Courtesy of Hong Kong Tourism Board; **7c** AA/B Bachman; **7cr** AA/B Bachman; **10tr** AA/B Bachman; **10tcr** AA/B Bachman; **10/11c** AA/B Bachman; **10/11b** AA/B Bachman; **11tl** AA/B Bachman; **11tcl** AA/N Hicks; **12** AA/B Bachman; **13(l)** AA/B Bachman; **13(ii)** AA/B Bachman; **13(iii)** AA/B Bachman; **13(iv)** AA/B Bachman; **13(v)** AA/B Bachman; **14tr** AA/B Bachman; **14tcr** AA/B Bachman; **14cr** AA/B Bachman; **14br** AA/B Bachman; **16tr** AA/A Mockford & N Bonetti ; **16cr** AA/B Bachman; **16br** Courtesy of Hong Kong Tourism Board; **17tl** Courtesy of Hong Kong Tourism Board; **17tcl** AA/D Henley; **17cl** Courtesy of Hong Kong Tourism Board; **17bl** Courtesy of Hong Kong Tourism Board; **18tr** Courtesy of Leisure and Cultural Services Department of Hong Kong; **18tcr** AA Stockbyte; **18cr** Courtesy of Ocean Park Hong Kong; **18br** AA/B Bachman; **19(l)** AA/B Bachman; **19(ii)** Courtesy of Hong Kong Tourism Board; **19(iii)** AA/B Bachman; **19(iv)** AA/B Bachman; **20** Courtesy of Hong Kong Tourism Board; **24l** AA/B Bachman; **24/25t** AA/B Bachman; **24/25c** AA/B Bachman; **25t** AA/B Bachman; **25cl** AA/B Bachman; **25cr** AA/B Bachman; **26tl** AA/D Henley; **26tr** AA/N Hicks; **26c** AA/N Hicks; **27tl** AA/N Hicks; **27tr** AA/A Kouprianoff; **28l** Courtesy of Leisure and Cultural Services Department of Hong Kong; **28tr** Courtesy of Leisure and Cultural Services Department of Hong Kong; **29t** Courtesy of Leisure and Cultural Services Department of Hong Kong; **29br** Courtesy of Leisure and Cultural Services Department of Hong Kong; **28br** Courtesy of Leisure and Cultural Services Department of Hong Kong; **30l** AA/A Kouprianoff; **30r** AA/N Hicks; **31tl** AA/N Hicks; **31tr** AA/B Bachman; **32tl** Courtesy of Ocean Park Hong Kong; **32tr** Courtesy of Ocean Park Hong Kong; **32cl** Courtesy of Ocean Park Hong Kong; **32cr** Courtesy of Ocean Park Hong Kong; **33t** Courtesy of Ocean Park Hong Kong; **33cl** Courtesy of Ocean Park Hong Kong; **33cr** Courtesy of Ocean Park Hong Kong; **34l** AA/B Bachman; **34tr** AA/B Bachman; **34cr** AA/B Bachman; **35t** AA/B Bachman; **35bl** AA/B Bachman; **35br** AA/B Bachman; **36l** AA/D Henley; **36/37t** AA/D Henley; **36/37cl** AA/D Henley; **37c** AA/D Henley; **37cr** AA/D Henley; **38l** AA/B Bachman; **38/39t** AA/B Bachman; **38/39c** AA/B Bachman; **39t** AA/B Bachman; **39c** Courtesy of Hong Kong Tourism Board; **41–42t** AA/N Hicks; **40b** AA/B Bachman; **41br** AA/A Kouprianoff; **42bl** AA/B Bachman; **42br** AA/N Hicks; **43t** Courtesy of Hong Kong Tourism Board; **44t** Courtesy of Hong Kong Tourism Board; **45t** AA/N Hicks; **46t** AA/B Bachman; **47t** AA/B Bachman; **48t** AA/B Bachman; **49t** AA/B Bachman; **50t** AA/B Bachman; **51** AA/B Bachman; **54tl** AA/N Hicks; **54tc** AA/D Henley; **54tr** AA/A Kouprianoff; **55tl** AA/N Hicks; **55tr** AA/B Bachman; **56tl** AA/B Bachman; **56tc** AA/B Bachman; **56tr** AA/B Bachman; **57tl** AA/B Bachman; **57tc** AA/B Bachman; **57tr** AA/B Bachman; **58tl** AA/B Bachman; **58/59t** AA/B Bachman; **59tr** AA/B Bachman; **60t** AA/B Bachman; **60cl** AA/N Hicks; **60cr** AA/D Henley; **61t** AA/B Bachman; 61cl AA/B Bachman; **61cr** AA/B Bachman; **62t** AA/B Bachman; **62/63c** Courtesy of Hong Kong Tourism Board; **63t** AA/B Bachman; **64tl** AA/B Bachman; **64tr** AA/B Bachman; **65tl** AA/B Bachman; **65tr** AA/B Bachman; **66** AA/B Bachman; **67–69t** Courtesy of Hong Kong Tourism Board; **67bl** AA/D Henley; **67br** AA/B Bachman; **68bl** Courtesy of Hong Kong Tourism Board; **68br** Sky 100 Hong Kong Observation Deck; **70t** AA/B Bachman; **71t** AA/B Bachman; **72** AA/B Bachman; **73t** AA/B Bachman; **74t** AA/B Bachman; **75t** Courtesy of Hong Kong Tourism Board; **76t** Courtesy of Hong Kong Tourism Board; **77** AA/B Bachman; **80t** Courtesy of Hong Kong Wetland Park; **80cl** Courtesy of Hong Kong Wetland Park; **80cr** Courtesy of Hong Kong Wetland Park; **81t** Courtesy of Hong Kong Wetland Park; **81cl** Courtesy of Hong Kong Wetland Park; **81cr** AA/B Bachman; **82l** AA/B Bachman; **82/83t** AA/B Bachman; **82/83c** AA/B Bachman; **83t** AA/B Bachman; **83cl** AA/B Bachman; **83cr** AA/B Bachman; **84tl** AA/A Kouprianoff; **84tr** AA/A Kouprianoff; **85–86t** AA/B Bachman; **85bl** Courtesy of Hong Kong Tourism Board; **85br** AA/B Bachman; **86bl** AA/A Kouprianoff; **86br** Courtesy of Hong Kong Tourism Board; **87t** AA/B Bachman; **88** AA/B Bachman; **89t** AA/B Bachman; **89c** Courtesy of Hong Kong Tourism Board; **90t** AA/B Bachman; **91** AA/B Bachman; **94l** AA/B Bachman; **94tr** AA/B Bachman; **94/95c** Courtesy of Hong Kong Tourism Board; **95t** AA/B Bachman; **95cl** AA/B Bachman; **95cr** AA/B Bachman; **96t** Courtesy of Disney; **96cl** Courtesy of Disney; **96cr** Courtesy of Disney; **97t** Courtesy of Disney; **97cl** Courtesy of Disney; **97cr** Courtesy of Disney; **98l** Courtesy of Hong Kong Tourism Board; **98tr** AA/B Bachman; **98cr** AA/B Bachman; **99t** Courtesy of Hong Kong Tourism Board; **99cl** AA/B Bachman; **99cr** AA/B Bachman; **100–101t** AA/B Bachman; **100b** Courtesy of Hong Kong Tourism Board; **101bl** © Steve Vidler/Alamy ; **101br** © James Davis Photography / Alamy ; **102t** AA/B Bachman; **103t** AA/I Moprejohn; **103bl** AA/I Moprejohn; **103bc** AA/A Kouprianoff; **103br** AA; **104t** AA/D Henley; **104bl** AA/D Henley; **104br** AA/B Bachman; **105** AA/B Bachman; **106t** AA/B Bachman; **106c** AA Photodisc; **107** AA/B Bachman; **108–112t** AA/C Sawyer; **108tr** AA/B Bachman; **108tcr** Courtesy of Hong Kong Tourism Board; **108cr** Courtesy of Hong Kong Tourism Board; **108br** AA/B Bachman; **113** AA/B Bachman; **114–125t** AA/B Bachman; **117bl** Courtesy of Hong Kong Tourism Board; **122cl** AA/B Bachman; **124bl** Courtesy of Hong Kong Tourism Board; **124br** AA/B Bachman; **125bl** AA/B Bachman; **125bc** Courtesy of Hong Kong Tourism Board; **125br** AA/D Henley

Every effort has been made to trace the copyright holders, and we apologize in advance for any accidental errors. We would be happy to apply the corrections in the following edition of this publication.

Titles in the Series